D0760398

Travel Deeper

A GLOBETROTTER'S GUIDE TO STARTING
A BUSINESS ABROAD

Ryan Spiegel

.

Disclaimer:
The names throughout this book have been changed in order to
respect privacy. The contents in this book are based off my experiences,
opinions, and advice. Please keep in mind that every country has
different laws and regulations so use my advice as a guideline.

Dedication:

I want to dedicate this book to my parents who have supported me throughout my life. They've given me the confidence I've needed to follow my dreams.

I also want to thank everyone who made my experience of opening a business abroad possible- from guests, friends, staff, locals, family, and anyone I had the pleasure of meeting during my time in Nicaragua.

Acknowledgements:

A huge thanks to Natalie Snyder who helped transform all of my experiences and advice into this amazing book. You were a pleasure to work with, and I know this will only be one of many projects for you in an amazing career.

Thanks to Sarah Feldberg for your great eye in editing this book and providing us with the mentoring we needed.

The amazing illustrations throughout the book are credited to Erica Halse. I am honored to have your work bring my stories alive.

I want to thank Ryan Hizer for creating an eye-catching cover for this project.

Thank you Ashley Duvan for your creativity and friendship throughout the years.

Table of Contents

"We read, we travel, we become."

— DEREK WALCOTT, THE PRODIGAL, *A POEM*

Intro

*"I don't want to end up simply
having visited this world."*

— MARY OLIVER

You know how a repetitive sound can bring comfort and calmness simply by droning on? Maybe it's the buzzing fan in your bedroom or the chattering dialogue of that TV show you've been binging on Netflix. Have you ever sat next to the ocean for hours, realizing your breath has deepened and your body has relaxed?

Well the sound of 10-odd chickens clucking behind your head on a crowded bus at six in the morning isn't one of those sounds. The redundancy doesn't become a lullaby. In fact, it only grows more irritating as time goes by. The sun rises, and the bodies sitting close to you become sweaty under its rays. The air begins to feel heavy with humidity, and you grow weirdly territorial of the squished spot that you're inhabiting, as if you're the only one entitled to the sliver of air within it.

It was the first time I had ever gone to Managua in a bus instead of a taxi. The price difference was significant: $7 per ticket compared to the average $80 round-trip cab fare. I was trying to rein in my spending now that I was living in Nicaragua and not just passing through. It was easy to justify dropping $80 on a taxi when I knew I'd be going home in a few weeks or a few months. Now the plan was to live here indefinitely, and I currently had no income.

Overall, I had been adapting to my new life rather well. I was naturally detoxing, fighting the humidity with two or three showers a day, sweating out everything I put in my system. Nicaragua was the cheapest sauna I had ever visited, and sometimes I felt like I was living in a sweat lodge. I consistently began my days earlier since the sun rose high in the morning, and getting up early made me feel more like an adult, which made me feel like I was doing something right, which made me feel successful, which made me feel slightly less terrified to be investing so much money into a business that, realistically, I was unsure would succeed.

Though I had been adjusting to my new environment well, this $7 bus ride was simply un-adjustable.

Between the chickens squawking and the relentless sun, everyone around me seemed irritated and deeply uncomfortable. Wedged into a window seat between the vehicle's skin-melting metal siding and a gentleman even sweatier than I was, I felt the same. I had hoped the fresh air would make the journey more bearable, but little did I know that nabbing a window seat also meant you were first in line for anything flying by that window, like, say, the projectile vomit from the woman in front of you.

Speeding along, a funny thing happens when someone vomits out the window: That vomit makes a complete 180 once airborne, only *really* affecting the person directly behind the vomiter. The vomiter comes out clean, and the bus keeps moving, no one even glances to see if the vomited-on is about to become the next vomiter. No one even offers a tissue to wipe the slimy, hot mess off your face or the inevitable tears of overwhelming sadness that combine with salty sweat and even saltier stomach bile.

I was 24, covered in a stranger's vomit, and I was about to open my first business in Nicaragua.

Hi. My name is Ryan Spiegel, and I'm here to tell you about all my experiences as a business owner in a foreign country. I won't try to convince you to open a business exactly the way I did (please, learn from my mistakes); I'll simply help guide you as you open yours.

My dream was always opening a business abroad. From the moment I started traveling, I saw the potential to create something impactful and successful, but psychological walls and financial hurdles held me back time and again. That was, until I finally stopped making excuses and committed to turning my goal into a reality.

In 2011, I co-founded a hostel in San Juan del Sur, Nicaragua - a quaint, beautiful surf town on the Pacific coast. Together with my partner, I grew an empty house into a profitable business from the ground-up. Literally. The hostel actually started with mattresses on the floors. Eventually we expanded to include a bar and restaurant, a surf company and an event business, along with an amazing atmosphere.

Over the years, I've been asked numerous times by people from all over the world how I did it. How did I actually open a business abroad and turn it into a thriving, money-making company? This book will answer that question. I'll recount the mistakes that I made and the lessons I learned along the way. I'll share my triumphs and trials and show you how you can open a business abroad too. If you're an aspiring founder seeking a new scene, if you're feeling stuck in your office job, if you're just ready to have a laugh at all the vomit-soaked situations I've gotten myself into, this book is for you. And I'll be laughing right alongside you.

Self Discovery

"I was surprised, as always, by how easy the act of leaving was, and how good it felt. The world was suddenly rich with possibility."

— JACK KEROUAC, *ON THE ROAD*

There's a restless feeling that starts to surface when I know it's time to travel again. It's a rush of anxiety that flows through my whole body and makes it hard to focus my mind. I always feel scatterbrained and impatient, sometimes irritable. There's a calmness that comes over me when I'm in the process of traveling. Nothing else has satisfied that feeling as well.

So what do you do? You keep traveling and traveling. And one day you start to contemplate how you can really travel *deeper*. My answer was opening a hostel in Nicaragua.

But let's back up for a moment.

I grew up in the San Francisco Bay Area, California, living in the suburbs and spending my childhood playing basketball and football with neighbors and classmates. I went into college confused about what I wanted to do with the rest of my life, but felt drawn to a business lifestyle. That way of thinking came easy for me, and it felt right. When I found out I could concentrate in Sports with a Business degree, I was set.

The next several years at University of Oregon were some of the best of my life. It was a time for complete independence and exploration. Oregon was full of beautiful deep greens and misty skies, and I fell in love with the place as I breathed in its heavy, refreshing air. So much so that I had a hard time deciding to study abroad in Argentina a couple years later during my junior year.

At this point, I had done a lot of traveling, but I hadn't exactly experienced *living* abroad. I was used to settling in an area for a week at most and then moving onto the next; settling down wasn't really part of the agenda. Traveling had satisfied my interest in different cultures, but spending a semester in Argentina allowed me to become immersed in the local culture and lifestyle. Buenos Aires was my first taste of living abroad, and it only left me wanting more.

In the past, my friends and I had joked about opening our own hostel. We primarily stayed in hostels so we could afford to extend our trips and so we could meet other young people who were doing the same. After a while, traveling didn't feel like a vacation so much as a lifestyle. We stayed in areas longer and got to know the rhythms of our adopted neighborhoods, the bus schedule, the best lunch deals, and the local grocery store. Traveling felt more like home, and we developed a sense of comfort and contentment. This feeling only deepened while I was in Argentina. Staying in one place for a little while was blissful, like the feeling you get when you melt into your chair after a long exhale. When you travel, you're physically moving from one place to the next, but when you hit pause and let your heart catch up, that's when you're finally completely present.

That feeling was always hard for me to walk away from, and I kept going back to it. After a while, I became obsessed with finding a way to make it permanent.

"How?" I asked myself. "How can I make that feeling a reality?"

Well, I'd have to eventually reside in an area that I considered my home away from home. I'd feel like I was traveling while simultaneously settling down. And I'd have to make it financially sustainable. In the past, when funds got low, I'd simply pack my bags and head back to California.

But this time I wanted to stay.

I needed to find a way to have a real income abroad. The businessman in me ran through different career moves that could bring in enough income to travel and give me the flexibility to work from anywhere. The more I racked my brain, the more I came back to one simple solution: I would work for myself.

While the idea was simple, the execution certainly would not be. Being your own boss and running your own business requires so much more attentiveness and dedication than your average 9 to 5. But the naïve, 24-year-old me decided I could make it as easy as I wanted. I was a capable and motivated young adult; I could open a successful business. So just like that, I made it happen.

Well, maybe not just like that, but it got the wheels turning. I began brainstorming how I could fulfill this dream. Where could I go? What kind of business could I open? What would actually work?

What came to mind? That joke with my friends about opening a hostel.

Hostels had been one of the most consistent details of all my travels, and the businessman in me loved to sit back and analyze what was working and what could be done better. I had an innate confidence that I knew what would make the perfect, thriving hostel. I had been to so many. I had seen different styles and themes. I had taken notes of how the buildings were laid out, what I left really admiring and, even more so, what I didn't.

While the mental notes piled up aside the scribbled notes in my travel journals, I realized I had already designed my ideal hostel, from the bunk beds to the common areas to the colors of the walls. And now that I'd built the perfect one in my head I wanted to make it tangible and real.

Of course, dreaming up the big idea is the easy part. The hard part is following through. For being a pretty well-traveled person, I can assure you I know how it feels to be lost. No, I don't mean literally, though that's to be expected when traveling; I mean lost in the beautiful chaos of life.

I know how it feels to be reluctant to shut the door of your childhood and walk through the one designated for adulthood. I know that hallway in-between. I know how it feels to write and rewrite a resume and to interview for dozens of jobs with only a handful of callbacks. I know how it feels to stare at a cubicle wall, scaring yourself with how well you know each flaw in the surface. I know how it feels when you start drowning in the mundane routine of everyday, when your internal clock's ticking haunts you as it grows louder.

Don't get me wrong, I love everything about my journey up until this point. I can't see myself ever changing that outlook. But that doesn't mean there haven't been numerous nights I've stayed awake wondering what the hell I'm doing with my life.

For me, settling into that ideal, cookie-cutter office job that provided financial stability and all the benefits of a comfortable life, well, that sounded more terrifying than traveling in an unfamiliar country. The idea of committing to a life of Monday through Friday with two weeks of paid vacation a year made me feel like I was suffocating. Scarier still was the idea of becoming comfortable in that routine and waking up one day to see a 60-year-old version of myself in the mirror. It literally kept me up at night.

Until I realized that that was okay. Instead of obsessing over the qualities I didn't have, I needed to embrace the lifestyle I craved.

The truth is, that office job, that career you've been building, it's not going anywhere. It's always going to be there, in some form or another. Being an adult doesn't just consist of having responsibilities and making smart choices. It also means making mistakes and learning from them. It means taking the right risks when you're ready.

So, let's talk about fear. What are you afraid of? What scares you? Make a list. (No, really, make a list on a separate piece of paper right now.)

Odds are, I've thought about every single thing you've written down.

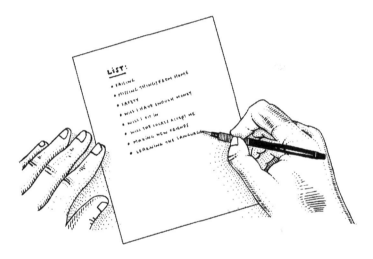

Now ask yourself, where is that fear coming from? Is it societal pressure? Maybe you don't want to disappoint your family. Maybe you simply don't want to fail. Is it money? Do you need more or are you afraid of losing what you have?

All these fears are legitimate and shouldn't be treated as petty. They're valid and real and all things that you should be worrying about.

If you *weren't* apprehensive about opening a business in a foreign country, then you'd be a bit of a fool. But being scared is no reason to give up on the idea of starting a business abroad or succumbing to a job you can't stand. Take some time to evaluate the things that have been worrying you, and try to see all sides of the potential situation. Don't be negative or discouraging to your plans. However, it's important to be realistic too!

The key is finding a balance of optimism and realism. You need to find the balance between childish excitement and mature responsibility. Analyze the situation. Weigh the pros and cons.

And don't be surprised when things go wrong.

It's inevitable. Your car is going to break down in an inconvenient place. You're going to hire someone who ends up being incompetent. Your computer system is going to shut down when the power goes out in town, and you most definitely will run out of toilet paper. It's all part of having a business and especially having a business abroad. These hurdles can be frustrating at the time, but in retrospect, I find them to be part of its charm.

So, embrace the fear, and tell yourself that the uneasy feeling in your gut is nerves wrapping themselves around something beautiful and worthwhile. They're just trying to protect something you so strongly desire. They come with the package.

That's the reason I decided to write this book, because I've been scared. I've had the same doubts and concerns. I've laid awake at night wondering if I'm going to lose all the money in my pocket to a failed business. But I've also laid awake at night telling myself another day in an office job would be the death of me.

I'm not here to tell you to plan everything to a T, and I'm not here to discourage you or feed you false hopes about how it's always going to be rainbows and butterflies. I'm simply here to tell you that your dream is possible. I'm here to help you think of things you might not have considered, to inspire you to follow your heart, to lead you to find comfort in the most uncomfortable situations and to share my stories in the hopes that you will take something away that could benefit you and your future business.

I'm here to tell you to take the risk. Save some money, quit your job, go on an adventure.

Go on another and then maybe more. Breathe in new air, put your feet in a different part of the world. Go on a trip where your bus breaks down in the middle of nowhere. Figure out how to communicate without a working phone or the best language skills. Love every moment of it. Feel your self-confidence build, feel more empowered and more adaptable.

Those are skills you'll take with you wherever you go.

And most importantly, you'll learn about yourself along the way. It's easy to lose sight of what's important to you and what makes you the person you are. Traveling helps make the space to focus on the essence of one's life. It excuses us from unread emails and fashion trends. It allows us to simply be.

So, before we go any further, it's time for some self-reflection. Who are you? What do you want to do?

I'm not looking for an answer. Not right now. I just want to get you thinking—about who you truly are, about your morals, your beliefs, your values. About what makes you happy, what makes you sad. About what you want to do with your days and with whom you want to spend them. What makes you feel alive and what makes you tick?

Find some time to slow down and just sit with yourself. Think about what moving abroad would mean. What would you love? What would you miss? Think honestly about your strengths and weaknesses and how those might fit or not fit with your future business. Remember that the coolest part of opening your own business is that *you* are the creator and thus a part of you is intertwined within it. Think about what business you want to live and breathe.

The hardest part of opening a business abroad isn't signing a lease or learning to run payroll. The hardest part is deciding that you really want to do it and taking the first step in that direction. So, are you ready to get started?

Location, Location, Location

*"I may not have gone where I intended to go,
but I think I've ended up where I needed to be."*

— Douglas Adams

I bet you love beaches.

Why do I assume that? Simple: a lot of people love beaches. Acknowledging what you like and where you find intriguing isn't a bad place to start when deciding where to launch your business.

Think broad. What areas of the world interest you? What cultures? What climates? Get a little more particular. Do you like coastline or mountains? A city or a small town?

Listen to your raw interests, because, well, that's probably a big part of why you want to have a business abroad, because you want to be somewhere new.

Of course there's more than surf access to consider when choosing a location. What is the area like politically? How is the economic climate? Is tourism a major industry? Is it growing? Will your business be welcome? Will you be safe?

How to Pick Your Country

Hey man, I'm going to be coming through Bocas del Toro in about a week. I was hoping we could get some beers and talk about the hostel business. Rob and I have been talking about the idea of opening a hostel one day, and I would like to talk to somebody with experience. I'm currently making my way up through Central America. I started in Colombia, and I should be hitting Panama very soon.

Ryan

Hey Ryan!
Awesome to hear from someone who's interested in this kind of life. Drinks on me – we'll have a lot to talk about. Hope California is as beautiful as I remember it... I need to make it home one of these days.

Sam

had spent the past year working with my favorite basket-ball team of all time, the Golden State Warriors. I had moved back to the Bay Area after college, back in with my mom with a goal to save as much money as I could.

At this point, I was 23 and had been toying around with the idea of opening a hostel for a while. At that age, goals and dreams change by the hour, so I never felt comfortable putting all my eggs in one basket. Like recent graduates, I had no idea what I wanted to do with the rest of my life. So, I decided to use that time to work my ass off and save money with the intention of following through with something – even if I wasn't sure what it was yet.

And, come on, I was working with my favorite basket-ball team in my favorite place in the world. So I have to say, I was pretty damn happy.

Still, throughout the year, the idea of settling anywhere gave me the heebie-geebies, and moreover, I was getting antsy to get back on the road. I love my mother dearly, but damn, living back home after you've been on your own for years is really difficult. Days spent on the couch watching *Seinfeld* reruns inevitably put me in a "what am I doing with my life?" funk.

With that in mind, my good buddy and I planned a trip to Eastern Europe. It was just an opportunity to get away and explore an area that I knew close to nothing about. During that time, I confirmed that I wanted to be abroad. I was drawn to the Latin American culture, so I bought a one way ticket to Colombia with plans to scout out potential landing spots.

I was starting to think seriously about opening the hostel, and I realized that I was in serious need of some genuine alone time, quality one-on-one time with myself. I was facing a big transitional moment in my life, and though I didn't exactly feel clueless, I still needed a little motivation to figure out which path to take.

So I started in Bogota, Colombia and decided to work my way up to Belize, stopping in Panama, Costa Rica, Nicaragua, El Salvador, and Guatemala along the way.

I had reached out to friends who might have any advice or connections in Central America, and only one person knew somebody down there: my future business partner, Rob, who had a family friend living in Panama and running *his* own business.

And guess what it was?

Yep. He owned a hostel.

The next few months went by with each day more fulfilling than the one before. The worst that I experienced never ended up being that bad. I got lost, confused, robbed and exhausted. I stayed in some questionable places, and my diet consisted of mainly rice and beans, but at the end of the day, there was nothing that a cold beer and a swim in the ocean couldn't fix.

I traveled from Colombia up through Central America with spots to stop and explore roughly mapped out along the way. Being flexible was crucial. Discovering the truly memorable corners only came from walking the streets and actually being present. I've found that I always want to stay longer in the places I didn't know about, skip the places I thought I would want to see and never have an itinerary for more than a few days ahead of time. Learning to "go with the flow" is vital; especially in a developing country.

And then I finally arrived to the palm trees and white beaches of Panama. I had packed a fresh notebook and extra pens, and I was more excited to meet Sam and pick his brain than for anything else on the entire trip. The more I traveled around Central America, the more I felt at home. The idea of living in this type of environment with my own business just felt … right.

Sam greeted me with two beers and a smile like he was seeing an old friend. I went to school for business and had worked in professional environments, so I could feel myself tense as I suddenly noticed how filthy my clothes were. I was totally unprepared for a business meeting, but Sam quickly made me feel comfortable.

Over the next few hours, we shared beer after beer. We talked about San Francisco and the rest of California. He had been living abroad for a few years and hadn't had many chances to go back for a visit. I could tell that had taken a toll on him. I gradually worked up the confidence to ask him the questions that had been circling my brain for the last year.

They ranged basic—"Why Panama?"—to more detailed—"Where did you buy your beds? How much of your supplies did you need to ship from the U.S.?" He kindly answered all of them, happy to share his advice.

He told me all about why he wanted to open a business in a different country, how he decided on a hostel and how he found the means to make it a reality. Most importantly, he told how he decided *where* to open his business.

"Ryan, listen to me. I can't emphasize this enough," he said. "You need to find exactly where you need to open your business. You have to find *the next big place.*"

The next big place.

He talked about the flow of tourism, local competition and how you want to be as close to the first person in a promising area as possible.

Sam had come to Bocas del Toro, Panama when it was still a busy local city without much tourism infrastructure. He could see that tourists would be attracted to the area and jumped at the opportunity to be one of the first businesses offering accommodations. If he was one of the first hostels in the area, he'd be sure to get a lot of business.

He also spent a lot of time speaking about Costa Rica. A lush and beautiful country tucked between Panama and Nicaragua. For years Costa Rica has been known for its tourism. It has beautiful blue waters bordering golden, soft sand. It has flourishing foliage that makes the inland areas as charming as the coastline. Its people are jovial and helpful, and many even speak great English.

It's known for its peaceful mentality and its national motto, "pura vida," which translates to "pure life" and is meant to emphasize the beauty of life and how one should take advantage of it.

But Costa Rica is also expensive. It has more surf shops, yoga retreats and resorts than you can count. You spend just as much, if not more, on a meal at a restaurant there as you would back in the states.

Costa Rica is not the "next big thing." It's the big thing. Has been for years. At the time, Sam was opening his business, he saw a lot of potential in Bocas del Toro to attract tourists from all over the world. Just as he expected, he was right.

He emphasized the timing.

"Bocas del Toro was great for me, but would I recommend it to you now?"

He shook his head no.

The night ended in laughs, pats on the back and a hug. I walked to my room feeling exhausted but also lighter. It was a mix of the light beers and the sense of a weight being lifted off my shoulders. I felt my doubt fading and a sense of self-assurance that my dream was more tangible than I had imagined. There was nothing to fear. I was a smart guy, and I was capable. Not only that, but I was passionate.

I fell asleep the moment my head hit the pillow.

The Takeaway:

Sam's simple advice was some of the most influential I had ever received: "Finding the next big place" is your number one priority. Possibly even over where you'd ideally like to be. (You're opening a business, not building your dream home.)

When identifying the next place, ask yourself these questions:

- Are there already a lot of businesses in that area?
- Are there any chain hotels or restaurants already developed?
- Is it affordable?
- Is it easily accessible?
- Does it have charm?
- Is the culture accepting of other cultures?
- Do you feel safe?

After you narrow down some countries that have the potential to take off, filter your list by where you think you'd be happiest. Then take a step back and consider the economy, politics, culture and language.

Economics:

You're opening your business in a foreign country, and it's important to understand the local economy and the cost of living and doing business. Do your research. Understand the exchange rate like the back of your hand. If you're considering a developed country, prices could be even higher than at home. If you're looking at a developing country, your dollar may go a long way. And since you're establishing yourself there long-term, take note of the stability of the currency and its exchange rate. Where was it last year? What about over the last 30 years? Where do economic models predict it will go?

Look for an area that has been stable for a long time and is projected to remain stable in the years to come. The last thing you want to deal with is a financial crash in an unfamiliar economy.

The simplest ways to find information on a particular country is to research online or seek out a local consultant in the country. The laws vary depending on where you are, so it's important to familiarize yourself with the specific ones that will affect you. Remember that you'll be subject to taxes as a resident and a business owner. Find an area that welcomes tourism and is friendly towards businesses opened by foreigners. If you need help navigating the local laws and taxes—and you probably will— find a knowledgeable consultant to be your guide.

Politics:

As an American, there are definitely some parts of the world where I wouldn't feel welcomed. I'm a nice guy, sure, but it's not personal. And you don't want to open a business somewhere that you, and your customers, could become a target.

There are also some areas where I wouldn't feel safe. In fact, I have traveled through multiple places where I didn't feel safe or comfortable, and I wouldn't choose to live in those places for obvious reasons.

Political stability is very important. Nothing discourages tourism like an outbreak of violence or a coup.

So, where is the right place for you? Where can you rest your head every night with ease?

Culture and Language:

This might sound obvious, but choose a country where you actually enjoy the culture. You're going to be living in it everyday, not just passing through, so consider whether the local culture fits your business and lifestyle. Find a place that you really love and can connect with.

You also have to be mindful of the local culture and traditions in terms of business.

You and your business need to be careful not to overstep any boundaries in the country. This is something I've seen happen time and time again. I've even had to watch myself on a number of occasions. In San Juan del Sur, the local government questioned renewing our business license due to photos on social media sites of people partying at the hostel. I've also had to accept that business deals can take weeks and maybe even months to finalize, something that definitely tested my patience. It's easy to let your ego get the best of you and take control. However, this isn't your home turf and this isn't your culture. Be respectful of the locals and the way they do things. Welcome the differences with acceptance.

Language is also crucial. If you're moving somewhere that speaks a different language, how proficient are you? Are you confident you can learn the local tongue? What's your plan for studying? Will you take classes or find a tutor?

If you're totally unfamiliar with the language or having a extremely difficult time learning it, I would recommend hiring a translator or finding a local consulting company that is fluent in both.

Even if you do speak the local language, you need to understand it well enough to do business in it responsibly and make sure you're not being screwed over. Again it might be smart to have a translator or consultant with you during those important business meetings.

Beyond the business, becoming fluent in the native language is very important for establishing relationships with the local community.

How to Pick Your Town

The border between Costa Rica and Nicaragua was a representation of each country.

I hopped out of the air-conditioned car, green jungle spread out behind me, and walked down a paved road and out of Costa Rica. Where it hit Nicaragua, the ground turned to dry dirt. I crossed the border with ease, ignoring the hecklers who tried to convince me to buy the paperwork I needed for a small fee, when I could get it for free a few feet farther on. At this point, I knew better. I'd had enough practice.

Cars pulled out in all directions, and wind blew the loose dust into a light haze, making it difficult to figure out which direction to go. I soon realized that it didn't really matter. Instead of a taxi, I found a truck with a barred cage and a couple pieces of plywood serving as seats. Only a matter of feet from the border, I certainly wasn't in Costa Rica anymore.

The drive was bumpy, loud, windy, uncomfortable and the weirdest kind of relaxing. I had picked up a new talent and appreciation for finding peace in the most chaotic situations. After an hour of that mess, I arrived in my next destination: San Juan del Sur.

I had heard about San Juan del Sur from a group of backpackers at the hostel I had stayed at previously. They told me about the fun bars on the beach and how the town had some of the best pizza they'd eaten on the road.

With their recommendation, I made quick plans to stop and stay for a couple days. Little did I know, this is where I'd settle for years to come.

It was the best time of the day in Central America. When you move closer to the equator, the mornings become nonexistent. By 7 a.m., the sun is high in the sky, and it feels like noon. Early evenings, however, bring conversation-stopping sunsets. Vibrant oranges, pinks and reds flow into each other as the sun quickly melts into the ocean like an egg over easy.

San Juan del Sur is spooned right around a bay where one of the few paved roads meets the sandy beach. This was the road I decided to walk upon my arrival. A few restaurants bordered the shoreline, and they had mostly locals inside. Laughter flooded from each one as I walked by.

The sun was creeping lower, and I still carried my entire backpack. I worried about finding a place to stay after it was dark, but instead of dwelling on it too much, I decided to slip off my shoes and take a load off, literally, in the sand.

(Those sunsets are something I never tired of. I miss them every day.)

I watched as the horizon got all gooey and the sun dripped into the ocean. The hour after left the sky glowing with warm tints. I tied my shoes, put on my pack and set out to find a bed.

As I walked back to the road, I noticed I had been smiling without even realizing it. I liked it here. This already felt like home.

The busiest block in San Juan del Sur was lined with a couple restaurants and a pool house where the locals sat on windowless window sills with their pool sticks and Toña's, the Nicaraguan beer. A couple large women with grease-stained aprons grilled chicken on the sidewalk. The smell was intoxicating and I had to try it.

For two bucks I had a meal consisting of half a chicken, rice (arroz con pollo), beans, tostones (savory, fried plantains), a few slices of avocado, some shredded lettuce and a sliver of tomato. Simple and delicious. (Later, I would find it was this good, every time.) Even the curb felt comfortable and welcoming.

(Every travel guide will tell you to be wary of street food, especially in developing countries. I say, yeah, that makes a lot of sense. I also say to hell with it; try this stuff while you can. It's usually a delicious and authentic depiction of the country. And it's damn cheap too!)

And after I finished my last, filling bite, I remembered Sam. *"You have to find the next big place"* repeated in my head.

I could feel my face light up with excitement. Any bit of fatigue I had acquired after a long day had been shaken off from the endorphins.

I strolled back down the road I had come, smiling as I looked over at the ocean at least once a minute. Then something caught my attention that stopped me in my tracks. A real estate office.

I walked in the door, backpack and all, and said, "Hi, I'm interested in seeing some of your properties. I'm looking to open a hostel."

The Takeaway:

You need to fall in love. That's important. But let's be real. You also need to make practical decisions that aren't fogged by infatuation. Love isn't enough. You also need to find somewhere your business will work.

Proximity is key in so many ways. I learned this the hard way, and though it was a growing experience, being aware of this information going into the business would have been a huge help.

At this point, you have an idea of what type of business you want to open. Let's pretend you're opening a surf school (or go ahead and think about your future business). Ask yourself this about your location: What do I need close by for my business to be successful?

A surf school obviously needs an ocean, but not just any ocean. You need to do your research on specific surf locations. Where are the waves good for beginners? Are they consistent year-round? Is there gnarlier surf nearby for more advanced clients?

But you need more than swells nearby. These are some things to consider, not only for your business, but for your own well-being.

How close are you to:

- Supply stores (grocery, hardware, department, etc.)
- Distributors
- A mechanic
- A hospital (very important!)
- A paved road

- Public transportation
- An airport

This stuff might not seem like a big deal right now. However after a torn achilles tendon, a staph infection, multiple car malfunctions and several four-hour round trip runs for supplies, let me tell you, it is a big deal. A really big deal.

Now, think about who your customers are. Who are you catering to? Where are they from? What's their annual income? What are they looking for (and how will they find you)?

I had a hostel business in a tiny beach town in Nicaragua. I was catering to younger backpackers on a budget. San Juan del Sur was the first city after crossing the border of Costa Rica, so it was a hot spot for backpackers to rest and enjoy the nightlife and restaurant options.

Now that you've narrowed down your location based off the needs of your business and your clientele, let's talk competition.

- What's already established?
- What's lacking?
- If you want to open a business that's already established locally, like a hostel, restaurant or bar, can

you do it better than what's already there? How will you differentiate your business? (Be realistic, not overconfident.)

Don't be discouraged if there's already a business similar to the one you want to open. Just take note of how you could do yours differently and appeal to a distinct or broader crowd. Maybe your business could complement a competing business. If you're really set on a town, brainstorm how you can make it work despite the similar businesses around you.

When I decided to open the hostel, there were already a couple hostels in San Juan del Sur and more opened after me. When you're in a developing country, your relationships with other businesses can be quite different. Everyone communicates with each other to help one another—from where you can buy paper towels in bulk to discussing ideas on how to bring more attention to your business.

I was so lucky to have a support system within the local businesses in San Juan del Sur. A few other expats who had hostels in the town actually joined together to create a weekly pool crawl that stopped by a few of the properties. Entry wristbands benefitted all the hostels as well as a local charity, and attendees would buy drinks and food at each stop. Everyone was happy and everyone won. In fact, the event is still popular and successful today.

There's no need to shut out similar businesses just because they're the competition. Think of each other more as a team and find a way to work together.

Relationships

"The business of business is relationships;
the business of life is human connection."

— ROBIN S. SHARMA

Humans crave interaction. Even the most introverted, independent person is bound to connect with some-one. Regardless if we crave it, it's simply unavoidable, especially if you're going to own a business in a foreign country.

If you've traveled, you've likely grown accustomed to sitting close to strangers on planes, striking up conversa-tions at bars or asking for directions on the street. The chance encounters you have while traveling can lead to the most memorable moments in your life, or at least an interesting story and some valuable information. And if you've traveled with a friend or companion, you know that the challenges of navigating a foreign country can push relationships to the boiling point or bring you closer together.

One of the biggest lessons I learned while running a hostel abroad was the importance of strong relationships and clear, open communication. Whether I was talking finances with my business partner or telling employees my expectations for the day, communicating effectively was absolutely fundamental.

I learned that lesson the hard way.

Partners

First, I want to tell you about Rob.

Rob and I grew up together in California, bonding over our love of sports and our inability to stay still. During high school, we would take turns driving to football practice or playing video games at a friend's house. Summers were for staying busy all hours of the day. We spent a lot of time going to various team sport camps, and eventually getting our own part-time jobs.

By the end of high school we had truly grown up together, from getting taller to hitting the gym as a pair to try building muscle to making our first attempts at growing facial hair. Together, we sampled some of the worst beers ever made and tried mixed drinks that tasted like the smell of our mom's nail polish remover. Our senior year, our high school football team rallied together and won the regional championship. (That might not mean anything to you, but at the time it was a big deal to me.) It was my first taste of putting a lot of effort into something and feeling the payoff of success.

I think Rob and I got addicted to that feeling. We both broke out of our shells, and though I was always a bit more on the quiet side, I tapped into an extroverted part of myself that I had never found before.

Football also taught us to be okay with messing up. We had to deal with losing sometimes, and more importantly, we had to learn how to use those frustrations as motivation to do better the next time around.

Giving up was never something I considered, and that came in handy when I decided to open a business in a different country. The friendship he and I developed growing up with each other and losing and winning together, aided in the next phase of our relationship: business partners.

During the summer between graduation and going our separate ways for college—while other kids were taking trips to beaches and renting houses for graduation parties—Rob and I, along with a couple other friends, filled our backpacks, triple-checked for our passports and headed to Europe.

That trip was really when everything began. It was our first trip alone, and other than our flight to London and our train passes, we had done very little planning (the best way to travel, in my opinion). By the time we caught our return flight in Barcelona, we had spent time in Paris, Amsterdam, Germany, Switzerland, Italy and the south of France. At 18, the five of us felt like we had seen the whole world in a month.

Along the way, we stayed in at least 15 different hostels. We originally decided to book hostels because they were more in our budget and seemed geared to a younger crowd. Five dudes together is inevitably going to be rowdy, and we wanted to be in a place that would be more accepting of that.

We didn't realize we were also choosing to have way less privacy and to meet other travelers from all over the globe. Most places had rooms with bunk beds and communal kitchens and bathrooms. We had conversations over delicious ethnic meals cooked by fellow travelers. Some of the best Italian food I've ever eaten wasn't from an elegant restaurant in Florence, but from a barefoot Italian backpacker.

What had started as a practical decision became our favorite part of the trip. We heard stories and perspectives from people of all kinds. We formed fast friendships and made plans with our new companions as if they were part of our little group from California. The connections I had made with my football and basketball teammates back home were amazing, but they were different than the relationships I was forming with these people from all over the world.

The hostel life had made our trip as unforgettable and amazing as it was. So, naturally, the topic came up: What if we opened our own hostel one day?

We began thinking about how cool it must be to run a business with so much energy and personality. We envisioned intricate details about how the bedrooms would look and where the hooks should be placed in the bathrooms. We joked about our roles and where in the world we could see our hostel happening. We even talked about what colors the walls would be painted and what kind of food would be on the menu.

What we left in Europe as a passing conversation, would later become reality for me and Rob.

After that trip, I became obsessed with traveling, so much that it was almost hard to focus in college. Every year I set out to visit somewhere new, from Australia to Costa Rica to Argentina, where I studied abroad with Rob.

That semester was our longest trip away from home, and it became significant for us to be experiencing it together.

As Rob and I traveled, we inevitably saw some of each other's worst days, as well as some of the single greatest ones. By the end of our semester, Rob and I had visited Uruguay and Brazil, backpacked in Patagonia and Chile, and seen the southernmost city in the world, Ushuaia in Argentina. (The city is viewable from Antarctica—pretty fucking cool.)

Those months were full of beautiful hikes and adventures, complemented by the nightlife of Buenos Aires. I might not have taken much away from my college classes, but I left with a better grasp on Spanish and of Latin American culture.

Rob and I had also developed a better understanding of each other.

We had learned what got on our nerves about each other and what we cherished. I knew Rob like the back of my hand, and he knew all my strengths, and even more so, my weaknesses. We had enough history between us that virtually nothing could break us apart.

So, when I told Rob I was seriously thinking about opening a business abroad, he looked right back at me and said, "Let's do it."

If you're reading this, you're probably thinking about opening a business abroad. But there are significant factors to consider when trying to commit, and sometimes having a partner can make all the difference.

The first: It's fucking scary.

I had only been out of college for about a year when I decided I wanted to open a hostel. I would get excited thinking about it, envisioning it—standing in a brightly colored lobby, smiling, laughing with guests—and then I'd feel my stomach turn thinking about the logistics and how incapable I really felt.

There's going to be some planning that goes along with the process, and it's not always going to be fun. But that's not enough of a reason to discourage you from doing something you've always wanted to do. It's normal to be fearful of a situation when you don't know how it might turn out.

What's a way to overcome your fear? Going into it with someone else. I mean, think about it. Any situation that scares you is less intimidating when there's someone else there to experience it by your side. It's simple, you feel less alone.

The second: It can be expensive. How the hell are you going to afford to open a business in the first place?

Financing a business, especially somewhere with a different currency, is tricky. I grew up in an era when the economy was not at its peak, and the idea of spending a lot of money on something with no guarantee of return was, frankly, intimidating. So much so that I actually talked myself out of the business a handful of times before committing.

Maybe you're not rich or maybe you spent most of your salary on rent or cell phone bills, but splitting the investment with someone else can make the money coming out of your pocket less daunting. (Keyword: *less.*)

And then there's the last factor: companionship. Traveling is fun. Doing something out of the ordinary is fun. Doing it with a friend is even better. If you're getting serious about building a business from the ground up somewhere beautiful and interesting far from the familiar life of home, of course you want to bring your friends along. Why wouldn't you?

And just like that, Rob and I became business partners.

With him on board, the whole idea of embarking on this project seemed tangible, realistic and not nearly as intimidating as it originally had. Not to mention fun.

Over the next year, Rob and I really saw the rawest versions of each other. We saw each other at our lowest, most stressed out points and in the moments of pure bliss and awe at our own accomplishment and success.

Here comes the brutally honest part: Rob and I went from being childhood best friends to barely being on speaking terms.

Our problems began early. The excitement of opening our own business abroad affected us in different ways. For me, I felt such a strong sense of responsibility out of fear that something would potentially go wrong. For Rob, it seemed like he was in it for the ride and really living in the moment most of the time.

We built a lot of resentment toward each other because we hadn't made clear what our designated roles were. When I was drowning in paperwork, I felt like he wasn't concerned. When he was entertaining guests at all hours of the day, he felt like I didn't acknowledge his dedication. I lost trust in him when I noticed how he was prioritizing our money, running the business when I was not there and his sometimes faulty decision making. Don't get me wrong, I wasn't perfect by any means, but our relationship drifted apart due to the lack of communication. I kept my jaw clenched and my thoughts to myself, and it didn't take long for us to find each other tough to be around.

We both took a lot of the issues personally, and it affected our friendship severely. Instead of being able to differentiate between our business relationship and our friendship, both cracked under the pressure.

Rob eventually sold his half of the business back to me and went on his separate way. It was a very tough situation, and neither of us dealt with it well. Looking back, we could have done lots of things to prevent it. I wish I had simply verbalized or even written my frustrations to him, and I wish he had done the same for me. But you know what, we didn't, and I am here to tell you what I learned so it doesn't happen to you.

My falling out with Rob was only made worse and irreversible by us being young and immature. I can only speak for myself, but I know my stubbornness and entitlement kept me from being able to work through our problems effectively or salvage a relationship of any kind. Had these issues surfaced at this point in my life, they would have been handled a lot differently. (I think that's the part that bums me out the most.)

Even in the times when we hated each other, we both knew that the entire project would have been impossible without the other. And that makes every part, good and bad, worth it. We created something awesome together and that will never be taken from us.

Now let me introduce you to Jen.

Jen was my second business partner after I bought Rob's part of the business. Unlike Rob, who I had known since childhood, Jen and I became partners when I barely knew her at all.

Jen had been backpacking through Central America and found herself at the hostel during her stop in San Juan del Sur. She was full of life and brought such a positive energy to the hostel that even in my most stressful times, I was able to have fun. She extended her stay in Nicaragua and began volunteering as a bartender to stay for free. I had seen this kind of trade in many hostels in the various countries I had been to. For the guest, it's a great way to prolong your stay without spending too much money. For the business owner, if you're not filling those beds with paying customers, why not give them to people who love what you've created and don't mind working a few hours at the front desk or bar?

Jen fit into the team right from the start. In fact, a lot of people assumed she was one of the original founders, rather than a guest who'd become an important part of the staff. She had been involved in the business in its most unrefined form just days after opening, and her personality helped shape the hostel into what it is to this day.

Three months after she arrived, I offered Jen a management position. I was five months in at that point and exhausted to say the least. I needed someone to take charge of a handful of tasks so I wouldn't feel so weighed down. Hiring a manager allowed me to step away from the business more and find some breathing room.

My relationship with Jen had developed at the hostel, and our friendship revolved around our mutual interest in the business and love for the country. I was able to build trust with her over time while our friendship grew simultaneously. Business meetings between us flowed very organically, and it was as if the friendship was a pleasant bonus of working together.

After six months, I began to realize how much I trusted Jen when I made plans to go back to the states for a 10-day visit. In the past, I wouldn't have considered leaving the business, even for a day. I would have anxiously wondered how everything was going and probably assumed that something terrible was happening like a freak dry-season flood sweeping the hostel away.

A week can drag when you want it to be over. It can also feel like a blink of an eye when you don't want it to come to an end. In this case, a week felt like an eternity to leave the business, but not nearly long enough for the kind of rest I needed.

I carefully packed my bag, enjoying every moment thinking about wearing my Warriors hoodie and breathing in fresh, cool air. The comforts of home sounded better than ever before, and I was growing impatient. So impatient that I began to realize I hadn't even talked to my staff about my trip. I scrounged up some paper and jotted a quick "To Do" list, as well as a "Don't Forget" list, a "Keep in Mind" list, and a "Who to Call" list for each and any kind of problem that could surface while I was away.

I handed it to Jen, who instead of stressing about running the business virtually on her own for 10 days, smiled and told me how happy she was for me to get away and see my family. The tension in my body immediately dissipated and a sense of relief overwhelmed me. She handed me a Toña and continued to dance to the music playing.

I trusted Jen. I truly did. She loved that business just as much as I did, and communication came easily between us.

Once I stepped away from the business, I was able to really evaluate exactly what was working and what wasn't. The truth was, I was exhausted. I felt run down instead of empowered, and running the business on my own 24/7 was becoming unsustainable. Hiring a manager took a lot off my plate, and I always wish I had done it sooner.

Realizing how stress-free I felt while away opened my eyes to the idea of proposing a partnership with Jen. She was grappling with staying in Nicaragua or finally moving on, and I thought this would influence her to make a decision either way.

When I returned to San Juan del Sur, I felt refreshed and ready to get back into the business. Fresh eyes really have a way of changing your perspective, and a fresh mind has a way of organizing itself.

I asked Jen to be my business partner. Though hesitant and nervous, she eventually said yes.

The Takeaway:

Here's what I learned through opening a business with one of my oldest friends and eventually having a partner I met through work. These things are so important that I'm honestly not sure how I began the business process without focusing on them more.

1. Define your roles.

Rob was more outgoing and had the natural ability to attract people to our business. He was fun, energetic and a character. If people were to leave the hostel talking about its owners, they'd say, "Damn, the owner Rob is so awesome!" without even realizing that I was his partner.

My strength was the logistics, the ever-exciting business side to the business. The truth is, I didn't mind. I was very good at it. I simply had different strengths than Rob and different ways to make the business successful.

The problem was, we never defined our roles. So while Rob was crucial in gaining a following and helping our guests have an amazing time, he also was seemingly *on vacation*. While I was buried in bills, cost-analysis charts, and meetings with lawyers and consulting companies, he seemed to be living it up and partying. I had moved out of the country to work hard, but I felt like I was doing it alone.

The resentment we felt toward each other would have been avoided if our roles had been clearly defined from the start. Had I gone into the business relationship knowing that I would be in charge of all logistics and paperwork and Rob would be in charge of outreach, well, that would've been that. The problem was, we both assumed. Rob assumed I saw how important his customer outreach was. I assumed he would noticed I was overwhelmed with the logistics of the business and needed help. You can't assume anyone knows what you're thinking, and you can't run a business if you don't open your mouth to communicate. The best way to communicate effectively is to do it from the outset and not just late-night over beers.

2. Written Agreements

In order to effectively define your roles and deal with countless other business issues, the terms need to be written down. In a professional document. In a contract. This document won't only cover each person's roles, but every detail of how the business is going to be handled.

Contracts are a way to protect both of you. "Hope for the best and prepare for the worst" can be applied to this situation very well. If you're getting involved in opening a business with a friend, remember this is an entirely different relationship. Make sure you can communicate with this person well enough that making a contract won't come off as an insult. (If you can't agree to put everything in writing, that doesn't bode well for the future of your partnership.) Often times contracts even cover what happens if a person involved in the relationship dies. Sounds insensitive? Like I said, prepare for the worst and always hope for the best.

This is also a good time to bring money issues to the table. How much is each person contributing to the business from the start? Get that upfront and in a joint business account before you start. What happens if the partners don't get along? What are the buyout provisions? What if someone gets hurt and can no longer work? What if you want to take on a new partner? Money can be awkward to discuss and tricky to negotiate. Don't let that stop you. Make sure you have covered all your bases and have everything in writing.

If you're going to take anything from me and this entire book, please make this be it. Aside from the importance of establishing professionalism, you really don't want to lose a friend. Especially a best friend.

3. Communication

You've likely heard it before, but I'll say it again: Communication is key. In all relationships in your life. It didn't take me opening a business to fully realize the weight of this statement. It took a few failed romantic relationships, some arguments with friends and uncomfortable passive aggressive work environments before I noticed an obvious pattern.

However, establishing good communication is often easier said than done. Communicating often means you need to be vulnerable. It means being honest and speaking your mind. It means opening up not only to another person, but also to yourself. It's empowering when it works out, and it's humiliating when it doesn't.

Here's where I give you that advice that's easier said than done.

Shut up.

No, not your mouth, your brain. Tell that damn thing in your skull to pipe down and chill out.

What I mean is don't let your brain talk you out of saying what you need to say or working through an issue just because you fear the discomfort or the awkwardness that might come from it. So what? The amount of relief you'll feel is worth it. Let problems fester and you're likely to build up resentment toward another person as well. (Trust me, I learned that the hard way.)

That applies to all types of relationships in your life, but it's especially important to keep in mind in your business relationships. If you've been friends with your partner since you were kids, learn to separate the friendship from the business. Set up times to meet, and then more times to meet, because talking is key (don't let things stew and get problematic). Use the close relationship to your advantage. You're in business with your best friend, so trust that they'll be there for you no matter what issues you may have. If they don't, then the friendship isn't worth it and the business relationship isn't worth pursuing.

Think of communication as the first step toward resolution. It may not solve everything, but you won't get anywhere without acknowledging problems and talking about them.

4. Trust

Just like communication, trust is crucial.

Trust in this circumstance means being able to trust the intention and commitment of your partner. You need to trust that your partner is dedicated and invested in the business in a genuine and honest way.

You also want to trust that your partner is financially sound and responsible. Hell, you're putting a good chunk of money into something, and you want to be confident that the person you are investing with is also worthy of your investment.

Okay, so now I've told you about my experiences with business partners on two opposite ends of the spectrum. I've given you advice I learned from working with both. Maybe this has helped you decide whether to seek a business partner or how to move forward with one that you have. Let's not forget about the option of going into business on your own.

To determine if you need a business partner, ask yourself these questions:

1. Do I need their **money** in order to begin the process?
2. Do I need their **expertise** in order to become successful?

| YES | NO |
| Okay, proceed. | THEN DON'T. |

If you don't need something from a partner in order to be successful, then don't have one. This doesn't mean you'll have to take on an intimidating project by yourself, instead it opens you up to hiring people below you. For example, I hired Jen as a manager to take away from my workload. In retrospect, I wish I had done that from the start and even hired more levels of responsibility. This way you can ultimately control all major decisions without having to run every part of the business.

Finding the Right Help

During the course of my time in Nicaragua, I lost friendships and trusted people who didn't have my best interest in mind. However, I also met some of the most generous and kind-hearted people in the world and helped my new community in return for welcoming me.

Some days consisted of me fumbling over broken Spanish to tell the local employees what time to arrive for work, and other days I was getting myself into a lot of legal problems. Honestly, both were considered pretty normal.

Bosco

When Rob and I decided to open a hostel in Nicaragua together, we first had to find a house to transform. I had backpacked through Central America and spent a lot of the time in San Juan del Sur. I knew I loved the town and saw a lot of potential in a growing economy, but I didn't have the exact location nailed down for the business I wanted to open. That's where Rob came in.

Rob had been living in Nicaragua, working for the Peace Corps. He had traveled through the town of San Juan del Sur with his brother and also felt its pull. His brother had a friend who owned some property and said they were more than welcome to stay in one of them. When another group showed up to rent the same place out, Rob and his brother had to move camp. The second house was bigger than the last one and had a better view. It was a two-story, all-white, Spanish-style villa with colorful tiles decorating the rooms. You had ocean views from every room in the house as well as the pool.

When I told Rob about the business idea, he immediately mentioned this house. I was convinced I had to at least see the place for myself. So I booked my ticket, and before I knew it, Rob and I were in Nicaragua, gazing up at at a two-story house with white pillars that exposed the bottom deck and supported a second-floor porch. Its L-shape favored the view, so no matter where you were in the house, you were naturally facing the ocean. Every time I entered a new room, I could feel myself trying to smile, but my smile couldn't get any bigger. I envisioned guests on every level. I could see them socializing downstairs, dancing to music. On the second floor, I could see some in hammocks, reading books or looking at the sun setting over the ocean. I thought to myself, "If we can't make this work, then something is wrong with *us*."

Though the house wasn't occupied, it still had a *cuidador*, Bosco, who watched over the house like a caretaker. He was directed to show us the property and welcome us with open arms, and that's exactly what he did.

The next couple months were a blur of paperwork and slaving away to transform this property into our dream hostel. In the process, we took on Bosco as our *cuidador* full time.

We had been so busy and focused on the hostel, that a few months after my arrival I had only made one strong relationship with a local, and it was Bosco. In Nicaragua, you can't open a business without having a local on the paperwork of the corporation, so suddenly he was written into the very foundation of the hostel. This man was basically the name of the business and was also charged with watching over the house, making sure nothing shady was happening. That included things like people sneaking onto the property, stealing and basically anything related to taking advantage of the fact that we were gringos.

Rob and I had an easy relationship with Bosco. From the first day we met him, he was friendly and spoke almost perfect English. He was our first introduction to Nicaraguan culture, and he treated us as if we were his guests staying in his home. He would cook for us and insist on cleaning up afterward. He was an artist and pressed the idea of painting elaborate murals throughout the hostel. We thought having local, Nicaraguan art on the walls would be a perfect addition to all the other ideas we had spent years cultivating.

Bosco even helped us organize additional workers from Managua. He knew people who needed work, and we had work that needed to be done. We preferred supporting locals, and wanted to help the local economy while building our business; it was a win-win. The months went by quickly, and as our opening day approached, we scrambled to prepare every last thing. Before we knew it, it was a week before opening day. We had been so busy getting everything ready that we had met almost no one except Bosco. Socializing involved painting a wall or remodeling a room.

When I finally made the decision to move to Nicaragua, my Spanish was limited. I had taken a few classes in high school and during my semester abroad, and used the lessons I learned while backpacking through Central

America. I had started taking private lessons in San Juan del Sur in order to communicate with our workers better, but it had only been a few months, and I had quite a while before I'd consider myself fluent. And before they'd stop laughing at me.

So there we were, sitting inside our beautiful house, one week before the big day. I was perplexed by the contradictory emotions swirling in my head. I was nervous we didn't have every detail finished and worried about the outcome of our business. I was impatient to see whether or not any guests would show up at all, but more than anything I was excited. Excited to finally open the business we had worked so hard to create, excited to see the scribbled notes in my journal become a reality.

This was probably the last week it would just be us up here. It was quiet and peaceful, what the locals call *tranquilo.*

That was, until my phone started ringing with one of those ringtones that sounds like a video game out of the '90s. It was Bosco.

"Get out here right now!" he yelled in Spanish, continuing in phrases I couldn't understand and ones that I wish I didn't, because it was clear that something was very, very wrong.

Bosco had gone to a private beach somewhere with our brand new pickup truck. The truck was our first big purchase. It was going to be used to haul supplies as well as shuttle our guests from the hostel to town or beach. The truck was a necessary part of our hostel's appeal and convenience. And Bosco had decided to pick up some ocean rocks to decorate the yard.

I had stared at him blankly when he told me what he wanted to do and instead of prohibiting him I thought of the approaching sunset and how cold our Toña's were going to be in the new fridge.

"Hasta luego," I told him as I walked away, shaking the confusion of why rocks were really a necessity right now. "Whatever," I thought. "A cold beer sounds way better than wasting my energy thinking about this."

But now, Rob and I were scrambling to figure out where this mystery beach was. Luckily, our neighbors at the bottom of our hill seemed to understand where our careless caretaker had taken our only source of transportation, and thankfully they also had a truck. So we bounced around in the back of this pickup, passively soaking in the last of the beautiful sunset and cursing Bosco, our words swept away in the heavy air as our neighbors sped toward the beach.

When we arrived, Rob and I stared at our beloved truck stuck in the wet sand while the tide crept ever closer. By the time we reached Bosco, the back half of the vehicle had sunk deeper, and the edge of the ocean was tickling the tires with every wave.

Before too long, the bed of the truck was filling with saltwater, weighing it down more and more. Bosco sat in the front seat, sweating more than anyone I had ever seen. Most of it was from the many failed attempts at getting the goddamn truck out of the ocean, but I'm certain I saw the nervousness in his eyes. He didn't know me well yet and I think he was scared shitless of how I might react.

But there wasn't time for that right now. The tide was rising, and our truck was basically disappearing. Our neighbors pitched in, lashing the two trucks together with rope. Bosco and some other locals stood on either side of our truck as the neighbor's vehicle revved with all its power in drier sand. Our vehicle would lift slightly out of the soaked beach, making a sound as if it were suctioned to something. But then the neighbor's truck would need a break and ours would slip back into the same spot, plopping down with a loud thud and hammering itself deeper into the holes.

Eventually, the ropes began snapping. The water kept rising, and at this point four or five different trucks had come out onto the beach to help us. I was amazed by all the local support, even for a gringo who spoke minimal Spanish and hadn't set aside time to get to know the locals and their culture. I'm not saying I was happy about the experience, but it opened my eyes to the generosity and kindness of the San Juan del Sur community. I made a mental note to put in a greater effort, then quickly got back to pushing the passenger side door of the truck in what felt increasingly like a pointless effort. Three-quarters in the ocean, our pickup looked like a goner.

Somehow through some combination of rope, truck and foot on gas pedal, we finally pulled our vehicle out of the ocean. Saltwater was pouring out of every possible place, but there she was: free and shining from her intense spa treatment. Everyone screamed with relief, hugging each other and laughing as if it were all a big joke. I stood there, catching my breath for the first time in hours, and I couldn't help but laugh too.

Soaked from a mixture of sweat and seawater, I wanted nothing more than to go home and shower the whole night off of me. I climbed in the truck with Rob as Bosco appeared from the crowd, his smile fading quickly. Rob and I had nothing to say, and Bosco seemed to have forgotten every bit of English he knew. We drove home in silence.

After that, we started to keep more of an eye on Bosco. Living in a new country while also trying to open a business leaves little time to focus on the small stuff. Rob and I started realizing things had been going missing around the hostel. Bosco started showing up to work less and later and seemed disinterested in being on our good side. We started trusting him less and noticed other shady things happening. Just a week before opening we came to a tough conclusion: We had to fire our main contact in Nicaragua and the person who was the legal representative of our corporation.

The Takeaway:
Listen, things happen no matter how much you plan and prepare yourself. There's no doubt about that. You often have to make mistakes in order to learn something new.

Between the relationship with Bosco and the overwhelming kindness of the Nicaraguans who helped reclaim our car from the Pacific Ocean, I learned that I needed to take time to get to know the locals better and form honest and genuine relationships. I needed to sort out who had my best interest in mind and who was trying to take advantage of me, instead of jumping at the first friendly face and outstretched hand.

It's crucial to find someone you trust wholeheartedly with your business. I don't believe that people are simply bad, however they can be very deceiving. As a foreigner developing a business in a different country, you're in an inherently vulnerable position, and some people will try to take advantage of that. I've heard countless stories similar to my experience with Bosco, some much worse, so it's very important to find someone or some company that has your best interests in mind.

Trust is such an important factor in every relationship, and it's even more important when you're in a place where you don't know anyone.

As time went on, we realized the best route to establishing trust was to go through a local consulting company who could ensure we were going about our business the legal way.

Let me tell you about Chepe and then introduce you to my good friend Maria.

Chepe

His laugh was as contagious as his calm and collected energy. He would stroll into the hostel early in the morning as if it was 5 on a Friday afternoon back in San Francisco. I didn't quite get it, but he seemed to just really like his life.

So there was Chepe, helping himself to a cup of coffee at 7 a.m. most days of the week. Rob and I took an immediate liking to him even if we couldn't communicate fluently. Sometimes trusting your intuition is the best route. With our Spanish skills still lacking, it was our only choice.

I tried my best to judge Chepe based on his interactions with other people around the hostel to see if he was just schmoozing with us for a paycheck. It seemed like everyone lit up when he walked in. The ladies would all giggle and blush like he had just told a joke or was charming them, and the men would greet him with an exaggerated handshake, followed by a pat on the shoulder. He seemed close with everyone. There was deep respect from everyone who passed, and I couldn't put my finger on why exactly, but Chepe appeared genuine and totally real.

After the whole Bosco situation, I started second-guessing myself, thinking my intuition was faulty. I felt like I had been cheated on and would be a fool to try to trust anyone again. (That sounds dramatic, but it's true!) And it didn't help that the only reason I met Chepe was through Bosco.

I watched Chepe from across the room as he shared a laugh with one of the painters. I shrugged. I trusted him, and that was that.

I didn't know then what would happen over the course of the next year.

It was May, and though we had only been open a couple weeks, the utility bills were already flooding in. Moving from California to a developing country in my early twenties made it a bit overwhelming to read bills for a business. (There were multiple times when I asked myself, "What the fuck were you thinking?")

I stumbled out of the truck to the hostel, exhausted from a night of entertaining guests and a day of running errands for the business. The last couple weeks had been a blur, meeting people from all over the world, sipping on Flor de Caña rum and knock-off Coca Cola, swapping travel stories and learning that "cunt" was a term of endearment coming from an Australian.

Most of the guests were either asleep or lounging by the pool, sweating out the night before.

I sat on a stool next to the bar and laid out the stack of bills I had picked up, as if I needed anything else to add to my lingering headache.

The first bill I opened was our electricity bill. Though the days were sunny and bright, our guests liked to stay up late, using the lights and fans for hours.

"Holy fucking shit," I said out loud as I rested my forehead in my hands and my headache intensified.

The paper read $1,500 (up from $300 before the hostel had opened). For one month. For one bill.

I felt a hand on my shoulder.

Chepe stood behind me with the most serious face I had ever seen on him. He looked directly in my eyes, while I tried to muster up the energy to change my body language to read as something less stressed. My attempt must have been pathetic, because he only grew more worrisome.

He took the bill from underneath my elbow and examined it closely. His eyebrows furrowed while his eyes darted from side to side, reading quickly.

"Ah, mi amigo. Yo te ayudo."

I stared at him blankly. Mainly because I was too exhausted to think in Spanish.

"¿Qué piensas?" he said as he stared back.

"Sí, sí," I said after a few seconds, relieved someone was willing to help.

He took his hand off my shoulder, and I felt some of the tension leave my body. Things were going to be okay.

Like I've said, Chepe was a genuine and charismatic character. He was a likeable person, with very few qualities that got on your nerves. The husbands of the ladies he made blush didn't even seem to mind. Moreover, he knew people. The right people.

The next day, I came back to the hostel to find Chepe speaking swiftly to a guy I had never seen before. I walked closer, and the man looked hesitantly at me, but turned quickly back to Chepe. He was reluctant to carry on a conversation past a sheepish smile and "hola." Chepe and he nodded at each other, the man moving away without hesitation, clenching a few tools in his hand.

"Hola, mi amigo. ¿Cómo estás?" Chepe said with a smile from ear to ear, patting me on the back more aggressively than the day before. I think it was his way of saying, "Today is a new day, chin up!"

My trust issues left me curious about the unfamiliar man who had come to visit so early in the morning. I couldn't help but think something was up, and I didn't know how I felt about it. Chepe had become like a father figure in my short time in Nicaragua, and I was starting to get the courage to confront him about what he had up his sleeve. He explained to me that he knew a guy who could rig our electricity meter to run slower, resulting in a significantly lower bill. He reassured me that this was normal and that I wouldn't get in trouble.

The whole situation made me uneasy. This was nothing short of illegal, but I was now living in a developing country, not California. Nicaragua barely had roads and definitely didn't enforce traffic laws. How could they pick up on one lowered electricity bill out of all the residents of the populated beach town?

Rob and I gave him the go-ahead, though Chepe had already taken it upon himself to do it, anyway.

When the next month's bill came in totaling somewhere around $400, Rob and I were ecstatic. We thanked Chepe over and over and celebrated how much money we were saving.

Every month for about a year, our bill hovered around that same price, and every month we were just as happy. That was, until the men from the electricity company visited.

There was no phone call, no warning, no notice. Just a couple of professional chicos walking with confidence into our little world. In that moment, I didn't know who they were, so I greeted them with a warm welcome.

The conversation was quick and jarring. They handed me a notice of a $5,000 fine, saying we had been stealing energy and that we should be ashamed to be thieves in their country.

I didn't feel like a thief. I loved this country, and I was struggling just like anybody else. I was giving back—encouraging tourism, giving locals job opportunities. I was insulted by these men who seemed to question my integrity.

I told Rob and Chepe about the incident, and Chepe laughed it off as if it were a freak coincidence.

"They'll never come back," he said.

He claimed it was a scare tactic, an intimidation attempt. He was a Nicaraguan, and he understood his people more than I did. Once again we were convinced to continue doing what we had been, and we collectively decided to rig the meter a second time. I know what you're thinking—and I'm not denying it. I was a young fool, making more mistakes than learning lessons.

It didn't take much time for the electric company men to return. They handed us another fine, this time saying if we didn't pay both, the power would be turned off completely.

So there Rob and I stood. Over a year into the business, owing $10,000 in electricity fines.

Chepe tried to help us fight the fine, but after a while, Rob and I just paid and called it a day. And we realized the money we owed was about equivalent to what we would have paid had we never rigged the meter at all. So we went through the trouble of doing something illegal multiple times for literally nothing. A lot of pain, and no gain.

The Takeaway:

Let's reflect on how that whole debacle played out over an entire year. One year, 365 days of trying to be rebellious.

During that time we paid cheaper bills, made a bad impression on the local government, defied the law and later paid a giant fee that negated all the illegal shit we did in the first place. Did we end up back at square one? Not exactly.

Don't get me wrong, Chepe was a very charming and genuinely kind person. Rob and I had many great times with him, and I felt like he was a friend as much as an employee. He brought a positive energy with him wherever he went, and I feel like it affected everyone at the hostel in the best way.

When I look back on the situation, Chepe was never trying to intentionally sabotage the business. In fact, I believe he was legitimately trying to help us out. But sometimes it's a fine line between those you can trust and those you cannot. Sometimes people blatantly don't care about you, and sometimes even though they do well, mistakes happen.

Regardless of Chepe's intention, we made a very irresponsible and unprofessional decision. So here's the real takeaway: Just do things the right way. Don't cut corners. Don't try to outsmart the system. Because in the end, you don't save much of anything. Hell, maybe I could have gotten away with rigging the line for a little longer, but doing something illegal in a foreign country gave me anxiety all the time. For a whole year. Not worth it one bit.

There will be opportunities to take a cheaper route, but while you may save money, you'll also gain a handful of other potential problems.

If you want to be a professional, you have to work with other professionals. But first you have to find them.

Local lawyers and consulting companies can help you familiarize yourself with the local laws and business regulations. They're the advisors who can ensure you're doing things the right way.

Cue Maria.

Maria

I watched as she stepped out of her car. Her Nicaraguan skin was darker than all the tourists staying at the hostel. She wore a modest denim skirt, her hair curled with the humidity, and she carried herself on Havaiana sandals from the local markets.

I'll never forget the look on her face the first time she came to the hostel. She walked over, poised and professional, with nothing less than terror in her eyes.

I had met her only a few days earlier. I was meeting up with my Nicaraguan friend Claudia at a local bar in town, and she brought along her amiga and future business partner, Maria. It was nice to get away from the hostel for an evening and meet new people who weren't guests. Claudia and Maria were educated locals with big plans.

Their English was nearly perfect, and I could finally feel myself evolving from "cluelessly opening a business in a foreign country" to "efficiently communicating with the right locals who want to help you succeed."

Claudia and Maria sipped mixed drinks made with rum and fresh tropical fruit juices. I wasn't used to hanging out with business people in this fashion. Reggaeton played in the background, and every once in awhile Maria stopped what she was saying to exclaim how much she liked the song.

The chicas told me about how they were opening a consulting company in San Juan del Sur. Their plan was to help business owners in the community run their businesses efficiently and follow the local laws appropriately. They would specialize in accounting, proper permits, human resources and everything in between. The more they discussed their business model, the more I realized they were exactly who I needed. They knew business, they knew the laws and, more importantly, they knew Nicaragua.

I told them about the hostel and how busy and overwhelming it had been since the day we opened. They listened intently, in a way a friend does when you vent. We all agreed that in order for the town to grow, it needed more affordable tourist accommodations. Central America was full of backpackers who relied on cheap rooms where they could unload their smelly packs and walk around with their dirt-stained feet.

They began asking me questions, ones that, looking back now, I can't believe I hadn't asked myself. They asked about pay rate—something I was proud of. We paid our Nicaraguan workers more than the average wage. They asked about paperwork—having the workers sign a contract that stipulated their wage and benefits. They asked if I had factored in bonuses, vacation time, holidays. I told them that we had simply been paying the staff cash in an envelope every designated payday.

Their mouths dropped simultaneously. Maria and Claudia began speaking the quickest Spanish I had ever heard. After a couple rounds of rum cocktails, Maria' sassiness could not be contained.

She looked at me with piercing eyes and started explaining in English, just as quickly as she had been speaking Spanish, how much *mierda* (shit) I could get in. How the workers could go to the labor office and say that they were never paid. How we'd opened ourselves up to all kinds of issues.

The conversation left me sober, despite the amount of alcohol I had consumed. I needed to make a change, and it needed to be now.

I didn't sleep much that night, and by the time the sun rose the next morning, I had already sent Claudia a message saying I needed to meet with her and Maria immediately. It felt good finally asking for help. I started to realize I subconsciously knew I needed help, but I had been stubborn and reluctant to admit it. Just sending a quick note to Claudia had lifted a significant weight off my shoulders. I did need help, and I was on my way to get it.

My phone made its outdated jingle. It was Claudia. She and Maria met me and Rob at the local coffee shop a matter of hours later. We made rough plans for the business, and Maria agreed to come to the hostel later that week. Part of me wondered if she regretted the decision to work with the business before seeing it. I decided to keep my mouth shut and gratefully shake her hand. I silently prayed that she wouldn't disappear after visiting the hostel.

The music was loud, especially for 11 in the morning. Guests ran around with alcohol in whatever vessels they could find. The girls wore bikinis with torn tie-dye shirts; the guys wore board shorts and had all seemingly lost their shirts during their stay. Some girls were laying by the pool topless to avoid undesired tan lines.

I couldn't help but laugh as Maria walked closer. I imagined she felt like she had just discovered a different universe, where the citizens were extraterrestrial creatures with strange behaviors and customs. She walked cautiously, seeming to wonder if her house was elevated enough from our little business. Could these creatures break into locked doors? Were they a threat?

I laughed to myself at first, but then my stomach twisted with fear. If Maria walked out on me, how long would it take for something awful to happen and the business to shut down? I needed Maria and Claudia.

Her face lit up when she finally saw me, and she transformed back into the professional businesswoman she was. I wondered if she thought I might have seen her shocked demeanor as she moved through the wild guests. She shook my hand and greeted me with a big smile.

In that moment I knew I was helping her just as much as she was helping me. I was one of Maria's first clients, and I'm sure one of the most challenging. She helped me really start the business, even if I had already been open for eight months. Maria was a huge help, and I don't know where I would have been without someone like her. She became a close friend and advisor, a relationship that every business person should look for in a different country.

The Takeaway:

The truth is, had I not made a few mistakes with whom I was deciding to trust with the business, I probably wouldn't have stumbled upon Maria. And even if I had, I wouldn't have realized how much I needed her. But I'm damn sure glad I did.

The earlier you can find your Maria, the more efficient your business will become. It's just that simple.

When you've found an area where you're thinking about opening your business, do your research and find a consulting company nearby. If you can't find a consulting company, talk to a lawyer.

A consulting company is a person or team of experts that provide professional advice for a fee.

While a great consultant will cost a little more out of pocket, this is a business, and a business is an investment in itself. If you want your hostel/restaurant/cafe/surf shop/bar/spa/boutique/smoothie shack/yoga studio/ice cream stand to succeed, you need to make quality decisions, and you may need someone to guide you in the right direction.

The truth is, Rob and I didn't realize we were absolutely clueless as to how to open a business effectively until we had already done it. If I hadn't met Maria that one night in town, I'm honestly not sure the business would have made it. Those men would have probably visited me many more times throughout my time there, and I most likely would have been leaving with them at some point.

What exactly will a consulting company do for you? Here's a list of things that Maria helped us with, without which we might have crashed and burned:

- Business permits
- Finding distributors
- Locating specific products around the country
- Accounting
- Recruiting local employees
- Human resources and how to properly pay the local employees
- Marketing
- ANY PROBLEM I HAD!

Locals

The drive on the dirt roads back into town felt even choppier than usual after spending the entire day with the soothing rhythm of the ocean. The kids' laughter had subsided as their bodies swayed side to side, like being rocked to sleep while they held onto their surfboards like teddy bears. I felt the heat on my cheeks, knowing my fair skin had gotten burned in the high sun. The light was fading, but I kept my sunglasses on to block the dirt blowing in my face as the shuttle sped down the road. This was the kind of moment that I'd later really miss.

When I reflect on my time as a business owner in Nicaragua, I think of the times I welcomed guests from Europe or Australia. They'd come to our hostel because they heard about the good times and bellyache laugh-inducing stories. I remember my friends from home visiting, saying I was "living the dream." I remember the smell of the grilled chicken in the streets and sunsets that distracted the whole town.

But sometimes I have to remind myself that the unfamiliar, exotic country where I had established my home was actually a developing country. I remember the unpaved roads, the women riding on the front of their lovers' bicycles to get to work. I remember the impoverished areas where extended families lived all together in one small home, filled with young children, chickens, dogs, aunts and uncles. I remember the kids wearing dirty clothing as they played in the streets, screaming and laughing with their friends.

After a few months of living in Nicaragua, the smile that stretched across my face whenever I left the market began to fade. I began to see myself as just another privileged gringo manipulating the country in my favor.

The cost of living in Nicaragua was cheap for me, but I learned that the minimum wage was equivalent to around $200 a month. Even when multiple people in the household were making an income, it only covered the bare necessities. The more I learned, the more I wanted to treat my employees better. The more I treated them with respect and kindness, the more I received in return.

Those crowded one-room homes and bicycles on dirt roads were all they had. The reason I didn't see many Nicaraguans at San Juan del Sur restaurants was because they couldn't afford to go out to eat with their families or to meet their friends for a drink. The reason they didn't have houses on the hill with a view of the ocean was because it made more sense for them to invest in a smaller home in town where they didn't need a car to get around.

The majority of the locals whom I met were good people, generous and always smiling. Sure, I came in contact with a few I would have rathered not meet and a couple I shouldn't have done business with, but overall, I was one lucky dude.

As I grew closer with my employees, I started to see more of their families too. I allowed my staff to bring their young children to work if they were going to be unsupervised otherwise. In turn, I felt that sense of family I had been missing since moving so far away from my own. The kids brought an energy to the hostel that had been lacking, and they made it feel more like a family atmosphere.

That's when I had an idea, though seemingly small, that meant so much to them and even more to me: I started to organize a dinner or barbecue for all the employees and their families. Instead of them doing all the work—the cooking and cleaning that they did every day for our guests as well as their own families—we would do it for them. Sometimes we'd even treat them to a dinner in town since they very rarely had the opportunity to eat out.

This became a recurring event that happened every couple months, and I prioritized it as much as I did hanging out with my friends. Naturally, I got to know my employees and their children better. These kids were so full of life. They seemed as happy and carefree as I remember feeling at their age, though their lives were totally different.

After the first few months of being open, the hostel began to get even more involved with the community. We focused especially on the kids, donating all kinds of supplies to the local schools. We even distributed them ourselves so we could see the kids getting excited over a pen or a baseball.

We also sponsored a local children's non-profit in town, donating our trucks and surfboards to take the kids out to the local beaches where volunteers from the hostel would give surf lessons. Though I wasn't much of a surfer, I could hold the boards steady for the kids as they climbed aboard fearlessly. "Paddle, paddle, paddle!" I'd yell as I watched them be swept away with the rolling waves.

They fell often, but they also stood up way more than I ever did. I think when you're a kid, you learn easily from failure. As you get older, it seems like people fear failure, whether it's falling off a bike, applying for that dream job or asking out someone you think is out of your league. As a kid, failure doesn't seem to be as much of a concern. It just happens sometimes, and you keep moving, because, well, why wouldn't you?

Watching those kids fall off their surfboards and come up from the water laughing were some of the most important moments for me and the business. I left those days feeling re-inspired and fearless, like nothing could stand in the way of my dreams. I left realizing that only I had ever gotten in the way of my own success.

It's true that spreading kindness and doing things for others affects you just as much. Those were some of my favorite days in Nicaragua.

The Takeaway:

Not only did those kids remind me to be fearless, but they reminded me what it was like to be part of a family. I saw how happy they were to return to their parents after a whole day in the ocean, and I felt a sense of warmth in my life. Meeting young, independent people from all over the world was amazing, but sometimes I craved a family dynamic in my life and a sense of home. By allowing myself to be immersed in the town and its people, I became a part of the community and less of a tourist.

Building your relationship with the local community can do nothing but benefit you. It wasn't until I got involved that I realized how happy it made me to help the people in the area, and how simple gestures can go a long way. Aside from personal fulfillment, the business began to flourish with people offering to help when it was needed or referring guests to the hostel.

Maybe most importantly, if you've had the opportunity to travel, to see different countries and experience different cultures, it's safe to say you've had a privileged life so far. Maybe you don't have the highest paying job, but compared to people in so many parts of the world, you're pretty damn lucky.

When I've traveled I've always taken note of how different the lifestyles were compared to what I was accustomed to. I remember being intrigued and infatuated with each one. Experiencing the local culture is the essence of traveling. It's what makes a place you visit feel real, it's what connects you to somewhere beyond the all-inclusive resorts and tourist zones.

It's natural to compare your life to the locals. I couldn't help but wonder if I should feel bad for the children in San Juan del Sur. They didn't have new sneakers for the beginning of basketball season. They didn't have video games. But they also didn't seem to care. They had each other, and that's what mattered more than anything.

Living abroad can put what's important in life into perspective. In Nicaragua, I spent most days bumming around in a pair of shorts and a t-shirt with a cellphone that I carried only when tending to the business. Those were some of the happiest years of my life.

You have to remember you're moving to a place because you enjoy learning and experiencing different cultures. So now that you have the opportunity to be really immersed in one, welcome it into your life with open arms. Try to establish a balance of what you can bring to the local community and how they can support your business sincerely. Make it respectful and mutually beneficial.

Get involved in your new community. Befriend the local people and give respect willingly. Be open to inspiration when it comes and never underestimate the power of kindness.

Lifestyle

"We must always change, renew, rejuvenate ourselves; otherwise we harden."

— JOHANN WOLFGANG VAN GOETHE

So you've daydreamed about living by the beach and you've bought your one-way ticket. You can't imagine any better direction than the one you're heading. You're about to embark on the journey of a lifetime—a move outside of your comfort zone to a totally different environment. You're finally going to satisfy your wanderlust by going on a permanent vacation.

But it's not a vacation.

You have to realize this quickly; hopefully before you arrive in the country you've decided to make your new home.

I don't say this to sound negative, but to be brutally honest. For me, escaping the 9-5 meant I was winning. I was able to work for myself and do what I wanted. But I absolutely was working. Constantly.

So let's talk about lifestyle—the one you've day-dreamed about and the one that's realistic and ulti-mately, just as, if not more, desirable. Here are my stories and hard-earned lessons that could have shaped the future of my business had I taken them into consid-eration earlier.

Balance

My vibrating phone buzzed on the cushion next to my pounding head. It buzzed closer and closer until it grazed the top of my scalp. I felt like a saw was cracking through my skull. It was 7 a.m., and I'd never been good with hangovers.

The hostel had become my world over the last six months, and this couch (placed regrettably close to the front desk) had become my bed. I didn't even remember what privacy or a bed of my own felt like anymore. Comfort? What was that? It certainly wasn't waking up multiple times in the middle of the night for fear of drowning in my own sweat (which smelled eerily similar to rum and light beer).

The hostel had a private apartment on the second floor that Rob and I shared. It was a large, single bedroom and bathroom, with no privacy. His bed lined one side while mine lined the other. On the nights I tried to sleep up there, he would wake me up when he decided he was ready for bed too. It always seemed we were on different schedules. If I wanted to go to bed early after a long day of working in the sun, Rob was staying up late entertaining guests. Sleep had become rare, and I had transformed into a tropical zombie.

The phone buzzing above my head was my alarm, piercing my sleep and forcing me to get up and start the monotonous routine again. I hadn't had a good night's sleep in months and the days began to blend into days. I snoozed the alarm. I couldn't remember the last time I had left the hostel on the hill, and I began to realize how silly it was of me to move down to Nicaragua and essentially put myself under house arrest.

The housekeeper bumped into the couch while she swept dirt off the Spanish tile.

"¡Lo siento!" she said. I gestured back that it was fine.

I dragged myself off the worn couch and found the nearest stool to prop myself upright until I actually woke up. Guests were strewn about in the various places where they had finally decided, consciously or unconsciously, to sleep for the night. One girl was wearing sunglasses with her mouth agape. I laughed to myself. I loved it here, but my head was still pounding, and my brain knocked on the inside of my skull with its dehydrated fist, screaming, "Get some fucking water, you abusive jerk!"

I was burnt out—from trying to figure out this whole business thing, from spending my nights on a couch next to the reception desk, from just being chronically overworked.

I needed a vacation. Or at least to get out of the hostel for more than a couple hours. Or at least a bed in my own space. I started to yearn for my bedroom at my mom's house—with her nagging and knocking at the door repeatedly. I never thought I'd say it, but that sounded way more relaxing.

I even thought about how I should Google "hostels in Nicaragua," forgetting that one was already my home. How could I relax and be on a vacation that reminded me so much of the place I was trying to get away from?

I grabbed a glass of water and chugged the whole thing in one gulp. I refilled it and poured it over my face, trying to wake from the haze I had been living in the last couple months. I took a deep breath, opened my computer and started my day.

I had developed a checklist and routine of how to start each morning. Though I had taken to drinking quite a bit on a regular basis—it seemed necessary to entertain our guests—I still maintained order and a strong sense of responsibility. I was just way more tired than expected.

I was in my early twenties, but every morning I awoke saying to myself, "I'm getting too old for this."

The Takeaway:

At home, I wasn't the kind of person who enjoyed the 9-to-5 framework, and I couldn't have been more excited to escape it. Little did I know Future Me would turn those normal 40 hour weeks into an exhausting and unpredictable 60-plus hours a week. Some escape, eh?

Time is precious. Someone said that once, and they were really right. You need to prioritize your time well. Your business is important, but not more so than your sanity. Finding the right degree of work-life balance is crucial, especially abroad where you may not have friends or family to encourage you to take a break and take care of yourself.

For me the work-home balance was practically nonexistent, and I had no one to blame but myself.

I don't know how I didn't take it upon myself to at least find a bed. (Sometimes I wonder how I was so dense about the most obvious things.)

The key is being okay with stepping back from the business, hiring people below you, delegating responsibility, carving out time for you to get away and finding somewhere to get away to. I'm a bit controlling and quite the perfectionist, so when I opened the business, I wanted to be part of every decision and to have eyes on it at all times. That simply isn't sustainable. Hire good people, be a boss. You already are one, so act like it.

Back to the bed. Take this very seriously. Find yourself a bed that is in a separate room in a separate building on a separate street from your business. Think about that relief you feel when you walk in your door after being at work all day. You need that sigh. You need that space.

Health

'll never forget the moment I realized my body had changed during the time I had been living abroad.

Nicaragua was poor, and public bathrooms were only equipped with the necessities: a toilet, a sink with running water (depending on if water had been cut off in the town that day or not) and hopefully some toilet paper. Mirrors were few and far between.

That specific day, I was visiting a friend at his house. I went into the bathroom and glanced up at my reflection. I looked a bit older and also a bit larger. Nothing to really worry about, I thought. I hadn't been as active as I was at home. I spent the majority of my time at the hostel, visiting with guests, working and staying up late.

I looked down at the floor and noticed an electric scale. I hadn't seen one of those in I don't know how long. "What the hell," I thought as I climbed onto the outdated device with confidence. The numbers swiftly moved higher and higher, and my eyes had a hard time keeping up. Why was it still moving? Why was it still going *higher*?

I stood there in a silent panic. Twenty pounds? I had gained 20 pounds? No. Nope. No way.

My mind ran through justifications. Muscle does weigh more than fat. (But I hadn't worked out in forever. The heaviest things I lifted were items in bulk for the hostel at Pricesmart.) I wondered if I had grown taller. (I hadn't.) I looked at my clothes in hopes that they might explain why the scale had jumped. (I was wearing board shorts and a tank top. Even my flip flops were near the front door.)

I hopped off the scale and walked into the other room.

"Dude, your scale is broken," I said, knowing deep down that I was wrong.

Temporary denial was more appealing than acceptance at the moment.

He laughed and said maybe I had been enjoying paradise a little too much.

I thought about how different my life had become over the last couple years. It had been full of beautiful moments and unforgettable sunsets. Long days spent in and out of the ocean and enjoying the town's affordable restaurants. Gallopinto for breakfast, fried tostones for snacks, tacos, burgers and the best pizza I had ever tasted were staples. Not to even mention all the Toñas and rum poured on top of that.

I don't know what I expected.

I thought more about how I used to have some sort of athletic practice after school or camp over the summer. I thought about how I joined basketball leagues in college and went to the gym as a form of stress relief when classes were bogging me down. Being active had always been part of my life, and I had really lost sight of that while abroad. I had prioritized everything else before my own fitness. I felt like that was the adult thing to do. I had a business I needed to care for; I had guests I needed to make comfortable. I had a reputation to grow. I had to be successful, and going for a run or eating a salad just didn't seem worth my time.

I reflected on how I'd torn my Achilles tendon about a year earlier. That probably wouldn't have happened had I been exercising regularly and taking care of my body. Instead, I'd gotten injured and in turn had to stay off of it even more to heal.

Less activity, the same amount of eating and drinking. I'd given up my routine from home and settled into a new one that was far less healthy both mentally and physically.

So there I was, sulking on a couch, sitting in front of a fan. I looked down at my gut every once in awhile, feeling like I was making awkward eye contact with an unwelcome visitor.

The Takeaway:

I want to make this very clear: Moving abroad is not the same as traveling. That's what a vacation is for, and starting your own business even in some postcard-worthy destination is not a full-time vacation.

I guess you can tell from my story that I behaved like I was on vacation. Now, ask yourself, what do you like to do on a vacation? Be really honest.

My vacations and travels consisted of drinking a lot—both in quantity and frequency. I would eat big breakfasts and always try dessert. Vacation was for relaxing and treating yourself, acting like a tourist. But it's time to go ahead and accept that you won't be a tourist at this point. You're home. ¡Bienvenidos!

The expat lifestyle can be significantly different than what you're used to, as to be expected.

Maybe you have an exercise routine at home. Maybe you cook your own meals and eat healthy. Maybe you walk or bike to work everyday or hit the gym in the evening. Maybe you regularly go to a yoga class.

But that's home, not vacation.

The trick is merging the two lifestyles. Find your routine, find some structure. Find a place to practice yoga or explore new habits, like running, surfing or hiking. Eat your veggies, and keep yourself moving.

I've made a checklist of things to take note of while living abroad that will make your transition smoother and hopefully help you avoid a shocking encounter with a friend's scale.

Adjusting your diet:

- Where's the local market? Where's the best place to buy fresh fruits and vegetables? It might not be a grocery store.

- What's in season? What kind of food does your environment produce? One of the benefits of living abroad is sampling new foods and produce that never make it to the shelves at home.

- Do you have a kitchen? Can you cook for yourself? Adjusting to a foreign kitchen can be tough, so stay patient. Figure out how to make the most of your space.

- Are there restaurants in town? Street vendors? The best pizzeria ever? Support them, just not all the time.

Staying active:

- What's the environment around you? What's the local culture's approach to fitness? Is it traditional dancing or martial arts? Is it something that interests you? Use the opportunity to discover something new.

- How can you use the environment to stay active? Are there hills to hike? Oceans to swim? Roads to run? Use them! Find hidden gems that you don't read about in the travel articles online. Explore different trails and less populated roads and find where they lead.

- What about the weather? Is the cold keeping you inside? Is the heat keeping you from an afternoon session? Is the rain making the dirt roads slippery? Adapt to your new setting like you would back home. You might have to alter your old routines and be open to making new ones.

- Are there local gyms or fitness studios? Local sports leagues or regular pick-up games? If so, sign up or get involved! If it doesn't work for you, then try something different. Local leagues are a great way to learn about the local culture and have experiences that the average tourist wouldn't.

I lost the weight, by the way.

The Transience Problem

Another month had gone by. It had been one of the best. The small group of people who had been volunteering at the hostel were scheduled to leave today, and it was hitting me hard.

They had said they were leaving on multiple occasions (most people do), but had always postponed the rest of their trip, pushing that departure date back again and again. Many of our guests and volunteers had fallen in love with the hostel and the family that formed around it. It was a hard place to leave. These people, in particular, had become some of my closest friends in Nicaragua, and I dreaded saying goodbye.

Seeing your friends leave here was different than back home. There were no holiday reunions or summer vacations to look forward to, no hometown rallying point where you were sure to see each other again.

Here, if you met a group from Australia or Germany, odds were good they weren't coming back for a long time or ever.

Central America is known for backpacking. The countries are warm, close together and relatively cheap. You could fill a backpack with swimsuits, shorts and T-shirts and, with relatively low funds, embark on an extended adventure.

Most people arrived at our hostel with a transient mindset. They might stay in one place for a day, a week, a month or even several, but ultimately, almost all eventually bid their temporary home adieu. Unfortunately, many of those people became my close friends.

I tried to treat the group like they were any other guests. I tallied up their bill and waited for them to check out. They had a taxi scheduled in an hour to take them to Managua to catch a flight in the evening. I had already planned to stick a Smirnoff Ice in their backpack, so when they hit security, they'd have to get down on one knee and chug the whole thing. When someone did this to you, it was called, "being Iced." At that point, it'd be warm and taste really, really bad. I knew they'd see the humor, even if all the Nicaraguans rolled their eyes at them.

I had started putting up a bit of a wall with the people I met in the last couple months. I was getting tired of making friends then saying goodbye, never knowing if I'd see them again. Some days I felt grateful for being in a place where I could meet so many interesting people from all over the world. Other days, I just missed having consistent relationships.

San Juan del Sur was still an up-and-coming tourist area, so there weren't many foreigners living there permanently. I had made some Nicaraguan friends, but my Spanish was still not the best, and forming that strong bond was difficult.

But I had let down my guard for this group of Australians. And, in the big picture, I was glad I had.

The Takeaway:

Okay, that was a little sad, but that particular situation was a big eye-opener for me.

Before moving permanently to Nicaragua, I honestly hadn't even thought about the transient culture. I thought I would be happy welcoming new people into my hostel and my life week after week. I thought I was privileged to have the opportunity to meet so many different people with a mutual love of travel. After a while, though, I started to miss my solid group of friends.

The hostel developed the saying, "Where People Come and People Go" to put a light-hearted twist on such a difficult thing to accept.

The Positives:

Even when people come and go, there's still the opportunity to make genuine friendships. I met people who impacted me in more ways than I could've imagined before living in Nicaragua. They were important to my growth as a human, and for that, I wouldn't change a thing.

Along with the intoxicating friendship you make, you also learn lots of skills while running a business abroad. One that translates best to life back home is networking. Networking is definitely one of best skills you can polish, and now's the time to realize there's a whole craft to it. You have to be confident enough to let yourself be vulnerable. You have to perfect the art of talking about yourself without sounding self-absorbed. And if you're not much of a talker, well, you need to start talking.

Traveling and having a business in a different country gets your name out there in so many ways. Instead of networking in a single city, you're now connecting with people from different continents, who are heading in countless directions once they move on. Maybe they'll remember you when they're looking for someone to do [insert your skill here] for their business. Maybe they'll stumble across your card or that crumpled piece of paper with your name and email on it. Maybe it sparks a memory, and they get in touch. Maybe *you're* going to take a trip where *they* live. If nothing else, you might have a place to stay.

The Negatives:

Good friends are, well, really good. There's something to be said for the relationships you form with that person you grew up with or your college roommate. Maybe your brother or sister have been there for you no matter what. Are you a momma's boy? Daddy's girl? (It's okay, you don't grow out of those things, you just get older.)

Odds are, you're not taking all those people with you when you start your business. If you're lucky, maybe you're bringing one along for the ride. Not only is it difficult to not share your favorite moments with your loved ones, but it's even more difficult to try something big without a support network already in place.

The truth is, if you're opening a business, especially one that caters to tourists, you'll want to place it where it can be successful and profitable. Those areas attract tourists, people who are by definition traveling through or visiting for a limited time.

Of course, there will likely be plenty of people living wherever you decide to settle. You have the locals and natives to the area and maybe a community of expatriates as well. Connecting with the locals is going to be more difficult than if you were to move from San Diego to San Francisco. There's a culture gap, an experience gap and often a wealth gap and language gap too.

In some places you'll find a community of expats where you might fit right in among other people who've chosen an alternative lifestyle and are running businesses abroad or working for one. But in San Juan del Sur there were just way more tourists coming and going than expats living there.

I started seeing my business and the town as a revolving door. After a while, I expected it to keep moving, and it never failed to do so.

It was hard for me to really put in the effort to connect with guests or even volunteers, knowing that they'd just end up hitting the road soon. While it was awesome to meet so many beautiful people from all over the world, staying behind as they moved on took a toll.

It was an adjustment, but luckily (yes, luckily), it's easier to stay in touch across longer distances than ever before. We're often said to be too connected in our day-to-day lives, but for people who travel or live abroad, email, apps like Whatsapp and social networks like Facebook, make it possible to keep in touch with the people you meet while abroad.

You can see the photos from the rest of their trip and catch up on each other's lives no matter where in the world you or they are. It's not the same as having a beer on the beach together, but it makes the goodbyes a little less heartbreaking.

Business

---

*"People will only follow you if they see you're
ahead, are convinced you know the route,
trust you, and want to get there too."*

— PATRICK DIXON

L et's get down to business. Literally. I'm going to get straight into the advice for this section. Hopefully my stories have entertained you and made you more interested and more confident about opening a business abroad. I want nothing more than to motivate you to follow your dreams and reassure you that you are capable of taking on such a fulfilling and life-changing project. I did it. So can you.

Keep in mind these are all general concepts that you should take into consideration. You will need to dig deeper into each of these for your specific business, but these are here to serve as a guideline.

Ready to get started? Here's how to take the first step.

Getting Started

Passion

Abig mistake A lot of people make when trying to decide on a career is focusing too much on the job title and not enough on what you will be doing on a day to day basis. If you like the idea of being a nurse but hate working long hours, then you might need to reevaluate that career choice. When you build a business from the ground up, you are in control of creating your career, and of course, you need to base that off a passion of yours. Think about how you can turn your passion into a business by thinking beyond the most obvious answer. Maybe your passion is food. Running a restaurant anywhere is a grueling, tricky business. You could channel your passion into a gourmet market, a cooking school or foodie tours.

Start with your passion or passions, and then expand from there. That is the ultimate first step. If you already know exactly what kind of business you want to open, let's continue!

Experience

When you apply to any kind of job, related experience is usually required. There's a reason for that: It's valuable. If you apply for a job as a general manager in a hotel with a background as a server in a number of restaurants, odds are you won't be the most desirable candidate in the stacks of resumes.

The same concept applies if you're essentially hiring yourself and venturing into territory that might be foreign to you (in more ways than one). It's not just about being a business person. It's also about having a background in and understanding your specific business. Even if you haven't studied business principles, you've probably learned some valuable lessons through your previous jobs and applicable experiences. Have you worked in the industry you're entering? Were you ever in a management role at any of your jobs? Did someone in your family own or run a business?

This isn't a necessity, but it's something to keep in mind. It won't keep you from being successful, but the whole process will be easier if you know what you're getting into and the challenges you'll face. If I could go back in time, I would definitely have worked in a hostel as a manager before opening my own hostel. Beyond the technical experience, feeling the day to day life of the business will really help you grasp if this is the right move for you.

Drafting a business plan

Before you jump into anything, it's important to organize your ideas as much as possible. The best method for doing this is drafting a business plan, which will help you identify potential issues that could arise and prepare yourself accordingly.

Think of your business plan as the skeleton of your business. It gives the business structure and supports all the little details you need to keep in mind. For example, it can help you identify the costs that will be associated with starting your business, as well as focusing on opportunities to raise capital, marketing, operations and just general ideas.

Don't stress out over this if you don't have a background in business. There are tons of online resources to help you create and tailor a business plan to you and your business. I've listed a basic guide that might be helpful, but definitely go online and find a specific business plan that works for you.

Basic Business Plan:

- Executive Summary - Overview of why your business will be successful.
- Business - What will you offer/sell? How will you be unique? Think about various revenue streams.
- Location - Take a look at the country you are looking to establish in. History? Economy? Politics?
- Competition - What else is out there?
- Customers - Who is your target market and ideal customer?
- Marketing - How will you reach your customers? How do you plan to market? What techniques will you use?
- Management - How do you plan to staff your business and manage your staff efficiently?
- Operations - What systems will you have in place? Goals?
- Finances - How do you plan to fund your business? How will you keep track of your financials? When do you expect to see a profit? What are your potential costs? Build out a financial model forecasting sales and expenses.

Competition

Like I've said before, competition isn't always a bad thing. The trick is being knowledgeable about what's already in the area and understanding how to differentiate your business and make it work within the larger landscape.

I wanted to own a hostel. There were a couple hostels already in San Juan del Sur, but I never felt they threatened my business, and though I wanted to succeed, I never wanted to threaten theirs.

Though we had the same type of business, there were a lot of factors that differentiated us. We were located outside of the town, which had its pros and cons. It was easier for people to walk through the town to find a place to stay for the night, but no hostel in town offered the tranquil view ours did. From my experience traveling in different hostels, cleanliness was one of factors that would make or break my stay. I put a lot of effort into the service side of the business and made sure our cleanliness was top of the line. Our hostel also attracted guests who wanted to spend time together, and in turn, we created a family atmosphere unlike any other in San Juan del Sur. The positive environment was contagious, and everyone welcomed new guests with open arms.

As more hostels started to pop up in town and take clients from our business, we decided to team up with another hostel with similar values and actually refer business to each other. That's right, you can even work with your competition. Think about how you can create something mutually beneficial and ensure success for both businesses. If there is competition in your location, don't bail just yet. Analyze the situation and see if it would truly cause a problem.

Of course, being the one and only business of your type in the area is ideal. That's Business Basics 101. But that's not always going to happen. Look at your competition and determine if there's room for your vision to succeed. If not, it might be time to reconsider the location. If you're set on the location, then you'll need to alter your business plan.

Capital

This is one of the most important elements to getting off the ground. No capital. No business.

Let's start with the simple stuff. A bigger project is going to need more capital. Simple. If you want a hostel with bedrooms for your guests, that's one thing. If you want a hostel with a restaurant, bar, yoga studio and a surf company, that's another.

I recommend starting small, solidifying your foundation and then growing your business as time goes on.

Now, let's discuss five different ways to gain capital for your project.

1. Raise your own.

Really. In fact, I highly recommend building your own capital. This might add time to the project, but finding a way to raise the money needed by working and saving is the surest way to guarantee that there won't be any funny business involved or any hoops that need jumping through. Think about ways you can cut back on your expenses and put aside money for your business. Figure out how much you need, then set a realistic timeline for yourself. Keep in mind that launching your business in an affordable area will lower startup costs.

2. Take out a loan.

This is a common approach, because for many people, it's difficult to obtain enough money to get a business off the ground. I wouldn't rule this option out, but it is another step in the process and has some serious drawbacks. The biggest issue is that it won't really be *your* business until you pay the bank back completely.

Also, how's your credit? In order to take out most loans, your credit needs to be excellent. It's also very difficult to take out a loan if you have nothing as collateral. Do you own a house? Do you own a car? Many times getting a loan for a business in a foreign country is very difficult or impossible. It's a dicey system, and you're better off avoiding it all together in my opinion. Ask yourself if you *need* a loan in order to obtain capital, and if the answer is no, then move on!

There is also the option of taking out a private loan, essentially borrowing money from friends or family with some sort of interest rate and payment schedule. This can be much easier than a bank loan, but it can also ruin relationships if you're unable to pay the loan back. Interest rates are usually much higher with private loans compared to bank loans.

3. Take on investors and/or partners.

This one requires a little more business savvy. That shouldn't deter you, it just requires drafting a good business plan and putting everything in writing. If you succeed in locking down investors, you'll need to divide equity in return for their investment dollars. Again, this means instead of the business being exclusively yours (and your partner's), it now is partly owned by outside sources. There are active investors (who help run the operations of the business) and silent investors (who usually just invest for equity in order to profit from the business down the line and are not involved in operations). Working out the logistics and payment structure for this can be tricky. Every situation is different, so look into it carefully before committing.

If you are going this route, then you'll definitely need a strong business plan in place to gain the investment dollars and formalize the agreement. Please reference the earlier business plan section in the book and also consider looking online for sample business plans or working with an advisor to make sure you're protecting your own interests.

4. A combination (my route)
In the midst of all of this, it's important to remember that raising capital doesn't have to be so "cookie-cutter." To open my hostel, I used a combination approach.

I actually had an outside source purchase the property in Nicaragua. (The *property*, not the business. That's important to note.)

After the property was purchased, my business partner and I each contributed an equal amount to the business. Though the investor we had did not actually invest in the business directly, they invested in the growing potential the business would have on the property. There are lots of different configurations that can help you build capital, but I would just urge you not to let it get overly complicated.

5. Crowdfunding

During my time abroad, I saw many people use websites like Kickstarter and GoFundMe to raise money by soliciting donations. Often businesses crowdfund online, offering rewards or thank yous in exchange for different levels of donations. Someone who donated $10 might get a thank you card or an article of apparel with the business logo, whereas someone who donated a larger amount might get two free nights all-inclusive at the hostel. I would be mindful and use these sources wisely. Though the spectrum of projects being crowdfunded is wide, varying from expensive medical operations to filmmaking projects, it might be hard convincing people to donate to your business simply because you need more money.

I wouldn't rule this option out, but I also wouldn't depend on it entirely.

Revenue Streams

Like I said earlier in this chapter when discussing capital, a smaller project is not going to take as much capital as a larger one. Does that mean you shouldn't grow into a bigger business? Absolutely not.

Truthfully, having a small project with one revenue stream (for instance, just renting beds at a hostel) won't make your business profitable in the long run. In fact, you'll be lucky if you break even.

That's why you want to brainstorm and map out ideas for multiple revenue streams, different ways to bring money into your business. My business started out as a hostel, but as time went on, we developed a full bar and then a full restaurant. Later we sold merchandise and grew into a surf company as well as an event company.

That didn't happen overnight. It took some time before the hostel profited enough where we could branch out and invest in growing the business.

But even if this is something that will happen down the road, you should keep it in mind as a long-term goal. For now, make sure your business has the potential to be expanded one day. That's when you'll truly start to see a profit.

How can you add revenue streams? For example, if you're a yoga studio, in the future you could add athletic apparel, host workshops or trainings, or open a juice or smoothie bar. If you're opening a bar, consider adding a restaurant or hosting musical guests or other entertainment.

Pick your brain and then pick some more.

Picking your Property

Accessibility

Go ahead and add this to the list of "Things That Didn't Cross My Mind Before Opening A Business."

No matter where you are in the process of starting your business, step back for a moment and consider its accessibility. Think big picture and small.

We'll start big: How simple is it for your future guests to fly into the country? From there, how easily can they be transported to your town? Now let's get smaller: Is your business within the town or on the outskirts? Is there public transportation? Will your guests feel inclined to rent a car or a motorbike? Will they feel safe walking? Is a shuttle service to and from your business needed?

The house and property where I wanted my hostel was set in stone in my mind. I was in love with the space as well as the location, and I was pretty stubborn about keeping it that way. *(Keep in mind, I had decided to open the business in a considerably busy town in an area with a prime view. Sometimes paying extra to be in a high-traffic area with a breathtaking view is worth the extra cost in the long-run.)* The only problem: The hostel was located 2 kilometers outside of town up a very steep, rather long hill.

San Juan del Sur was full of taxi drivers, but the old cars couldn't make it up our hill. Not only that, but the locals had a tendency to take advantage of tourists and charge them extra for their rides. I didn't want my guests to show up at the hostel with a bad taste in their mouths before they even got to unload their bags and look at the view.

We quickly realized we needed to develop a shuttle service from our hostel to the town and back. It would be free to all guests and would run every two hours to take guests to and from the property. We fashioned seats out of wood in the bed of a truck and built a cage-like surrounding, so guests could feel secure on the bumpy roads. It wasn't the most glamorous form of travel, but that was part of its charm. Later, we used the same cages to transport surfboards to and from the various local beaches.

The extra supplies and service were an additional cost we didn't initially expect to dish out, however, I'm 100 percent positive that the shuttle service was the difference between my business being successful and failing. Yes, failing. It just goes to show how important this detail really is.

Now that we've discussed accessibility, let's decide if you should rent or buy the property. I took the route of having an investor purchase the property the house was on. This allowed me to rent directly from the investor, making the process quite a bit smoother than if I had been renting from a local who was uninvolved in the business. (At the time, I wasn't fluent in Spanish and was still very new to the culture.) Let's discuss what's best for you.

Renting

Pros

- Less upfront costs
- Less of a commitment
- Not locked in
- Big issues are dealt with by landlord

Cons

- Any modifications or improvements aren't to your property

- Rental agreement (time frame)
- Lack of control
- Dealing with a pesky landlord

Legal

I'm sure you've experienced renting an apartment or house, and I'm sure you remember signing the line at the end of the packet of papers you may or may not have read. (If you had bothered to read the fine print, you would've known that you couldn't have pets or a third roommate in that small room/oversized closet. Something you failed to pay attention to until after you adopted the puppy at the shelter with the biggest, saddest eyes. You've been there, I just know it.)

While you're likely familiar with a rental contract, when it's a business rental there are certain parts of this document you should take careful note of:

1. That they allow you to make the changes you want to the property for your business.
   - If you know you're going to want to build a fence or paint some walls, make sure this is okay with your landlord and that it is written into the contract.
2. That they are okay with the type of business you are running.

- o If you're opening a bar, but they think alcohol is poison, odds are they're not going to be a fan of your business from the start.

3. That they are okay with the hours of operation.
   - o Do they live on the same property? Do they wake up at 5 a.m.? Are you planning on having loud music play until at least 4 a.m.? I sense this could be a problem.

4. Length of the rental
   - o You want to have time to develop your business. You don't want to start something successful and then have to move to a new location because they won't renew the contract. You're probably used to signing single-year leases. As a new business, you need to keep in mind it will take at least a year to get your business up and running. You don't want to finally feel stable and secure after a year only to have your landlord say, "Ehh, it's not working out, and your contract is up."
   - o Strive for 3-5 years. Maybe even consider making an agreement that after the 3-5 years, the rent can increase a certain percentage. (Of course, if they don't need an incentive to rent the property to you, don't suggest this!) You

can also explore the option of a lease-to-buy type of contract on the property.

Side note: I also noticed that many locals who rented out properties would try to copy the business on that property after it had left or if the lease was up and not renewed. This was interesting to me because, though the business model was the same, it often failed. This really helped me learn the importance of branding your business and its name. Your business won't be successful just because you have a nice property with a view. You need to consider the atmosphere you want to create and what you'll put into the business to make it unique. Avoid depending on the location and physical appearance of the business to build your success; make it successful because of you. We will address this later.

Buying

Pros

- Build Equity
- Control
- Money invested increases value of property
- No landlord to answer to
- No/limited rent (depending on how it's financed)

Cons

- Any problems with property are *on you*
- It is a bigger investment and not as easy to step away if the business fails
- More capital to raise

Legal

Go ahead and realize that buying a house or property in a foreign country isn't going to be the same as doing it at home. They're simply two different places, and there's no universal way to buy property. I recommend really becoming knowledgeable in the legal system of the country. (For many reasons, but this is one of the big ones.)

Keep these things in mind:

- Make sure there is a title (one that is clean and clear)
- That it is a registered property with the legal system
- That no one else has rights to it or has money owed on the land

This is where you will want to spend a little extra money to make sure you have a good lawyer with your best interest in mind. Take the time to get multiple opinions from legal counsel before buying, and then double check everything you already have. It really can't hurt you to be overly cautious here. This is a big investment, after all. No funny business. No pun intended.

Neighbors

As I've said before, I was so wrapped up in my business at the beginning that I really never got around to meeting people or socializing. Dedication is important, however that was a huge mistake on my part for so many reasons. For one, becoming acquainted with the country, the town and the people is, without a doubt, one of the most important parts of having a business in a different country. In this case, it's not about just getting to know the culture and local people, it's about getting to know your neighbors.

I failed to get to know my neighbors very well, and unfortunately, I didn't get so lucky. My neighbors and I never saw eye to eye, and I never felt comfortable with them being so physically close to the business. They seemed to despise me and the hostel enough that I always worried they would find some way to jeopardize it. Clearly, it added unnecessary stress to the already extreme stress I had.

Basically, you need to be considerate of neighbors. Respect that they were there before you and will likely be there after, and genuinely prioritize time to befriend them. You want to make the impression that you've moved to be a part of the community and not there to take over. Your business should never make other people's lives difficult, so communicating with them about what you're starting and your intention is very important. That way nothing will surprise them, and if an issue arises, you'll have an open channel of dialogue and be able to address it.

Just go say hi, dammit!

The Legal Stuff

P ay close attention and get a good handle on the legal issues that will affect your business before launching.

It's important to note that these factors will vary depending on the country, state and even town where you start your business. If you're not much of a business-person, these issues may be very new to you, so pay attention. If you're already familiar with these concepts, well, pay attention anyway. It's still beneficial to have something to reference as a reminder for your next business-venture.

Taxes
How will taxes in your host country affect your business?

It's safe to say that taxes will greatly affect your business no matter where you decide to launch. My recommendation is to find a consultant who knows the country very, very well and take advantage of their expertise. I know I've already stressed this in earlier chapters, but it really should be one of your first priorities upon entering the country.

Can tax laws really be that different in another country?

Absolutely.

In my experience, Nicaragua's tax laws literally made no sense to me as a businessman. After studying business in college, I understood boring things like taxes really well. That meant I was even more confused after looking into the laws of my new country.

One of the strangest things I noticed was that you were taxed based on the amount of revenue you brought in and not the profit/loss. Let's say you make $20,000 over the course of a month, but after all of your expenses, your business actually *lost* money. Well, Nicaragua isn't concerned with that. You would still be taxed on the $20,000 in sales.

So what did I do? I paid it, obviously. The last thing I wanted was to have my business shut down due to unpaid taxes or taxes I didn't know existed. This is why it's important to not only find a consultant or accountant to help you understand the tax laws, but to ensure you're paying all the required taxes for the country.

Side note: Developing countries may have special tax laws that are very advantageous for potential investors. Discuss this with your consultant, because you may qualify for tax breaks!

Find the answers to these questions:

- Will you still have to pay/file taxes in your home country?
- How much does a good accountant cost?
- How many different taxes are assessed to my specific business?
- How often do I have to pay taxes? (Monthly, quarterly, yearly?)
- What are the tax brackets in the country? Tax rates?

Laws

When I first had the idea for this book, I reached out to friends and family and asked them what they'd find beneficial to know before opening a business abroad. The most consistent answer was "laws," and for good reason! So, I'm here to emphasize the importance of learning and understanding the country's laws (keyword: *understanding*).

Local laws can typically be found simply by using Google (bless you, Google). The trick is finding the most updated and translated version if you are not fluent in the native language. I also recommend talking to your local lawyer or business consultant about the laws that will affect your business. This way you can have a more *applicable* knowledge of the laws. Odds are, locals or people who have lived in the area for an extended time understand what the government really is opposed to and what is more accepted in the country.

Take that information seriously. Don't do anything you're not supposed to, because if you've ever seen *Locked Up Abroad*, that certainly isn't the route you want to take.

Permits

Please do not let this part of the business slip your mind. These are documents that need to be updated on a regular basis. In my experience, I had officials come into my business during peak hours and request to see certain permits. If they weren't up to date, they would have had the power to shut down the hostel right then and there.

This is another important thing to run by your consultant. Ask what specific permits are needed for your type of business and how to obtain them. You should expect to hear these mentioned because they are common in every country.

- Tourism
- Health
- Fire

- Police
- Government/local mayor's office
- Tax ID

Like almost everything I've mentioned above, permits also vary from country to country. Educate yourself on the potential permits using the Internet and then discuss them with your consultant once you get settled. I recommend keeping your documents well organized and finding a way to be reminded to update each one at the appropriate time. Don't let petty paperwork be the reason your business has to shut down.

Business Entity

So you've finally decided on your business, and you're ready to make it happen. What should be one of the first things you do to get the business up and running?

After finding your consultant, make sure you discuss starting a corporation.

Why, you ask? Think about it in terms of liability. Instead of the liability being on you personally, it's now on the corporation.

How do you become a corporation?

I can't promise it will be consistent for every country, however the process usually requires a local or someone with residency to be the legal representative. At this point, you probably haven't obtained residency and maybe you never will. As I've mentioned in previous chapters, it is very important to build your relationships with the locals and involve people you trust in the business. Once you've accomplished that, you also might be able to find someone you trust to be your legal representative. If you're not on a time crunch, I recommend taking the proper steps to becoming a resident. The downside is that it can take quite a long time. You can always start with a local legal representative and then take over that position once you have your residency.

Though I ultimately recommend opening a corporation, it could depend on the size of the business you're opening. Larger businesses often open corporations, while smaller businesses usually open under a single person. Depending on what type of business you're starting, it might be worth taking this route, because opening a corporation can be more expensive, especially as a foreigner. It's up to you to decide if it's necessary and worth your buck. For our purposes, larger businesses are things like hostels, hotels, bars, restaurants, whereas smaller businesses are surf companies, smoothie shops, etc.

There are obvious benefits to opening your business as a corporation, one of those being the liability being on the business rather than yourself. Also, it often reduces taxes and additional costs. You're able to open a business bank account when you wouldn't normally be able to open a personal one. Also, when you set up an account with a distributor, they're more likely to be lenient on orders and your credit.

Side note if you have a business partner: This is a great time for you to initiate working out a contract with your partner. Be specific: How much money are you each contributing? What is the ownership breakdown (50/50)? What are each person's roles? Make sure to include some nitty gritty clauses that spell out what happens if someone wants out of the business or, like I've said before, even if they die.

Human Resources

You've likely had some experience with human resources in previous jobs. Their role is to ensure that the people involved in a business or corporation are being treated fairly. They're the people who manage your bonuses, vacation time and even your hiring and training. Human resource management might cover similar topics in every organization, however it's slightly different from company to company. Now apply that concept to a different country.

Yep, you guessed it. Human resources people still exist, they're just very different. This is another topic to discuss with your consultant, and it's worth looking into right away.

If you remember the story of when I first met Maria, you'll recall how appalled she was at how the business was being run right from the start. I can even remember the pitch of her voice when she looked at me with big eyes, distressed by the fact that I had no records of my employees' pay for the first seven months. I guess I was claiming ignorance is bliss, but saying "I wasn't aware of the labor laws" sounded idiotic (even if it was the truth). That's when I really realized I needed to get it under control, and without Maria, I'm not sure I ever would have.

Luckily, Maria was able to help me backtrack so I could move forward with my business successfully. During those first months, I hadn't fired anyone and no one had quit, so I didn't have to worry about employees with ill-will trying to take me and the business under. I had taken really good care of the people who worked for me. I allowed them to have free meals on the job, free clothing if they needed, and I organized the family barbecues to make them feel appreciated. Regardless, I still needed to maintain the proper paperwork to avoid big fines from the labor board for unfair treatment or even court battles due to the undocumented wages.

Things to look into and remember:

- Vacation time
- Holidays
- Bonuses
- Hour restrictions
- Payment rules (minimum wage)
- Contracts
- Documented pay stubs/wages

Banking

The term "banking" obviously implies that a bank is involved, so I feel like it's necessary to inform you how difficult it is to open an account without residency. This is another reason getting your business set up as a corporation can be extremely beneficial. The last business move you want to make is justifying a safe full of cash in your bedroom. (What?! I've learned a lot from the time I started…)

Now that we've set up your bank account, let's have a little chat about currency.

You've done some traveling at this point, so you're aware of currency exchanges. You're also probably aware of how traveling in more developing areas is easier on your wallet, not only because it's just cheaper, but because the exchange rate works out in your favor. Often the money you make in a developing country would not support your cost of living in a more developed area. Even when you're profiting in the country, you may not be in your home country. It's just something to keep in mind when you begin your business abroad. Do you value profiting in your home country while abroad? Or are you just concerned with a humble living while abroad?

Residency

We've already discussed the benefits of becoming a resident and how it can aid your business, allow you to make your business a corporation, open a bank account and ensure you have a safe place to deposit your money.

I've also told you it can be a lengthy process with a lot of paperwork.

That being said, immediately begin the paperwork upon your arrival and meet with a lawyer you trust. Prepare yourself for many bumps in the road and practice everything you've ever learned about patience. The process will most likely require you to have copies of documents from your home country, so come prepared with copies of your passport, birth certificate, social security card, health certificate and police record ready to go.

Is it worth the wait?

In my opinion, absolutely. Since the process does take a while, you'll probably need to have a local become the legal representative of the business before you can officially become one. This was how I met Bosco, and this is a big reason I wanted to have my name on the business instead of his!

Having residency will make your life so much easier. Being the legal representative of your corporation, setting up bank accounts, putting bills and vendor accounts in your name, setting up permits and being the overall decision-maker eliminates middlemen and can help you retain control of the business.

Running the Business

Now that we have talked about getting the business set up, I want to bring up some points on running your business. This can range from posting flyers around town of your grand opening to whether you should have Christmas lights or tiki torches lining the yard. It includes what kind of systems to use to organize the business, as well as branding and keeping track of financials.

Marketing

An important and necessary part of every business, marketing promotes the product or services you offer with the intention of attracting customers. Though challenging, if done effectively, it will drive customers.

The marketing industry is evolving with the expanding use of social media, but keep in mind that in a less developed area, access to those networks sometimes just isn't there and things that work well at home may be far less effective. This will alter your marketing tactics, however an online presence is still key. Think of how you will reach people who have planned ahead or are still planning their trip. Maybe they're researching restaurants or places to stay. Maybe they want to go to the best surf school or camp. You want to be the answer to their search—highly visible, easily accessible, informative.

Either hire someone to build your website or create one yourself. There are many great user-friendly platforms for building a website. Check out Wordpress or Squarespace or find another one that you prefer. A polished website with beautiful photographs and clear, concise information on the business can make a huge difference.

Once you have your website established, set up social media accounts on sites like Facebook, Twitter, Instagram and Snapchat. These are great marketing tools for your business. You can use each one to accomplish a different thing. Use Instagram to post photos of the business and those enjoying it to attract future customers. Update your Facebook status about special events or job listings. Use Twitter to be part of the dialogue with guests both past and present, maybe even future ones with questions or concerns. Depending on the type of business you choose to open, you'll need to be mindful of booking or review websites such as Tripadvisor or Yelp that could review and rate your business. This is a great way to see feedback for improvements or positive reinforcements. Sometimes you'll have that jerk who had a bad day, but don't let him ruin yours too.

You also want to make your business easy to find when searched online. Search engine optimization, SEO, can be worth understanding if you're in a competitive market and want to be a top result of online searches. It also takes time to get established and move up in the Google rankings, so be patient. Always include the URL to your website on your social media accounts. That way if a client finds your Facebook page before your website, they can be linked to it from there and vice versa. Make sure your website has all the links provided for your social media profiles. The purpose is to stay connected, right?

Now that you're literally all over the Internet, let's talk about local, smaller-scale marketing.

If you're reading this book, odds are you're not in the middle of Paris opening a hotel. You're more likely in a more affordable area that brings its own marketing challenges.

A Facebook update might not get the message about your Friday night party out as quickly as you're used to. From my experience, I found word of mouth is huge. Simply telling someone who enjoyed your business, "Hey, tell your friends to come by," can be incredibly effective. In a lot of ways, it's more organic and honest, because it ensures your focus is on your guests and providing the best experience possible. I was a new business in an area where the clientele was primarily backpackers and those traveling through. This culture of travelers is so heavily based off word of mouth. "Oh, you're heading to San Juan del Sur? Be sure to stay at this hostel!" If this is going to be your clientele, expect to rely on word of mouth as your first marketing tool above everything else. So establish yourself and build those relationships!

More hands-on promotions are things like making flyers, stickers, signs and even advertising in the local newspaper. I took to giving out free merchandise to the locals, providing them with something they maybe couldn't afford and helping my logo be seen and remembered. Signs and flyers should provide clear directions to get to your business, so people who are making spur-of-the-moment decisions can find it easily. The more channels you are in the more people you will reach.

Operations

Maybe you're the most organized person in the world who has the memory of an elephant and won the mathlete competition every year in school. Good for you. I'm still going to recommend you have some sort of official system in place with software or programs that help you organize business data and keep track of sales. Considering the time saved and the stress avoided, an easily accessible system that is efficient and organized can only benefit the business as a whole. These systems can vary from business to business, but I definitely recommend spending the extra money to invest in one that suits your needs.

The size of your business and the amount of sales you have will help determine how much you need to spend on putting systems in place. Remember organization and checks and balances are huge. They will help prevent stealing and waste and will allow you to keep track of what's going on even if you aren't there all the time. It will also help you maintain good records, which are crucial for the financial side of your business.

Many systems can keep track of all the following items for you. Make sure to do your research and find one that suits your company's needs.

- POS - Point of Sale
- Inventory
- Reporting
- Finances
- Ordering/purchasing
- HR/payroll

Accounting/Financials

So the idea of crunching numbers doesn't necessarily sound like the most fun activity, but when it is directly affecting your business, it can be exciting to see what's working and how to gauge your businesses costs and profits.

In all seriousness, you want your business to make money to sustain you and your lifestyle. If you're not keeping track of your financial records, you won't know how close you are to reaching your goals, and you won't see areas for improvement.

Much like with your businesses operations, I recommend some type of system to keep track of your financial records. Many POS systems include records of sales, inventory and expenses and have a back-end accounting and reporting system. My experience mainly comes from using Quickbooks, which is accounting software. I think your best bet would be to stick to one system that includes everything you need for recording both your finances as well as operations. Of course, if you have a smaller business with fewer revenue streams, it'll be easier to keep track of your finances, but the larger the business is or the more it grows, the trickier it's going to get. Invest in a system while you're still small and watch the money trends from day one.

If you went to school for accounting or business, you might actually be familiar with using Excel spreadsheets efficiently, and though that's not a bad idea, it might be more confusing for someone with no experience. Find a system that will work best for your business and let it do the work of tracking your financial data. Make sure it is easy to use so you can train staff to use it properly.

Now let's fast forward to some future time. You've gotten the itch to move somewhere else or be closer to your family. It's time to look into selling your business. (Sad, I know. It hasn't even opened yet, and now we're selling it.) Let's get together all your financial records to be able to clearly show those interested just how successful your business has been. *Wow, so successful, would you just look at that! Oh look, they want to buy the business right on the spot. I'm so glad you took my advice on keeping your financial records.*

Okay, so maybe it won't exactly work like that, but you understand what I'm saying. You want to have the records to show that your business is worth buying and is a good investment.

Keeping these records is not only beneficial to you in the short term, to see your business grow from losses to eventual profits, but also in the long term to see the rate of your success and prepare for selling or moving away at the right time.

Or you can use a pen and paper.

Name/Brand

If there's one thing you want people to take away from your business and remember, whether they found you on Instagram or were a guest a year ago, it's your name. You want it to come up in conversation around a table of friends years after the trip. It should be something simple and memorable, even amongst all the unforgettable moments in your guests' travels.

Sure, you have your difficult-to-pronounce names, your names in different languages, your names that use "Z's" instead of "S's" or even the unique book or movie reference names. I stick with simplicity. Something short and sweet that evokes your business and something unique enough to stand out from all the brands crowding guests' heads. We actually thought of the name for our hostel years back when we were backpacking through

Central America and knew that it was simple, catchy and fun. People loved our name; it helped them remember us, aided with word of mouth and was huge to our success.

Naming and branding your business effectively will help your clients locate and remember you and increase the impact of merchandising and marketing. Hire someone to design a cool, original logo that, along with the name, establishes your brand identity.

Building a strong brand will also come in handy if you have plans to relocate or expand your business. The idea of opening another business in a different location shouldn't be as nerve-wracking as the first, especially once you've created a successful brand and made a name for yourself.

Merchandising

I've touched on this already, but let's talk about it some more. You've established your brand at this point, and you've built a logo around it. You've been marketing on social media and on flyers throughout the town. You've got clear, easy-to-read signs directing clients to your business. Local people are becoming familiar with your name and logo. Now let's try marketing in a more material way that can also provide an additional revenue stream.

People who travel love souvenirs. They especially love souvenirs from places they find memorable and significant in their time away from home. Since your business is awesome, your clientele probably wants to take a piece of it with them. They want something that can't be found in a department store or worn by everybody else walking down the street. They want something tangible, something unique. That doesn't mean it has to be something that's never been done before. It can simply by a T-shirt or a hat that has your logo and name printed on it, something only people who've been to your business can own.

My hostel eventually made stickers, patches, koozies, sunglasses, fake tattoos, hats, T-shirts and tank tops. There's no need to overthink or overanalyze what your business should produce. We were located in a tropical area, so T-shirts, tank tops, sunglasses and hats only made sense. Since our clientele were mainly backpackers, being able to purchase an article of clothing after wearing a lot of the same stuff for a long period of time was an amazing feeling. We also had a bar, so koozies were relevant and useful. Fake tattoos were a hit for girls in their bathing suits, and people bought stickers for their water bottles and patches for their backpacks. It all made sense, and everyone was happy to take a little bit of the business away with them.

You can use your merchandise for free giveaways, contributions to fundraisers or events or as an incentive for people to stay at your business longer. Open your mind and think outside of the box!

Atmosphere/Vibe

This might seem like the cherry on top, but in a lot of ways, it's the essence of the business and something that can make or break it. A business can have a perfect business plan and the most expensive furniture, but if the atmosphere and the energy of the place is lacking or cold, your guests won't connect to it nearly as much.

That's why it's important to establish a theme for your brand or business. You want it to be aesthetically appealing and draw people in. Invest in some decorations and be mindful of how you design the layout—where the couch goes, where the sun rises and sets and how to place decorations based off the lighting. If this isn't your strong suit, maybe your partner can help you or you can turn to Pinterest for inspiration. With the power of images on Instagram and social media, consider what photo opportunities you're creating. Do you have a cool sign for people to pose with? Will your space photograph well?

The second part is creating the right vibe, and that often comes down to hiring the right people. If you have an energetic, upbeat business, you want the people working for you to embody that. If you have a laid-back, relaxing environment, odds are that first person won't be the best match. You want your guests or clients to feel invited and welcomed into your business, and having staff that communicate that will make a big difference.

Moreover, I truly believe that hiring a mix of locals, expats and volunteers creates the best experience for both your employees and your guests. It's a way for everyone to experience different cultures and create an open-minded and harmonious environment.

So invest in the Christmas lights that stay lit even if one bulb goes out and don't forget the importance of throw pillows. (Also, learn what throw pillows are.) Hire mindfully and trust your gut! Make it fun and have employees fill out a short questionnaire that helps you identify their personality and if they would be compatible with your current staff and the business itself.

Most importantly, remember the vibe of the business ultimately begins with you, the owner. You have to set the tone for your business atmosphere, your employees and your guests. Make sure your staff knows what is expected from them, and make sure your guests know what to expect from you.

The Wrap Up

*"The world's big, and I want to have a
good look at it before it gets dark."*

— JOHN MUIR.

My plane from San Francisco to Houston was early. Over the last two years, I had flown back to Nicaragua five times, so I had a packing system that was flawless and an in-flight footwear strategy. The air blowing on my toes would make my whole body cold, so I wore sneakers for the first flight of the trip, then changed into sandals for the second leg, anticipating the Central American heat. I sat in the window seat looking out at the gray skies and the plane's wing dripping with cool rain.

It rained in San Francisco often, and though it made for relaxing afternoons with a movie, I was excited to get back to Nicaragua's dry days. I wanted the clear blue skies and the sun's warmth cradling my whole body.

Two years earlier I had sold the hostel to my business partner, Jen. I was ready for something new and a change of scenery. I missed my family and friends, changing seasons, cold evenings wearing a sweater, and afternoon walks that didn't begin and end drenched in sweat.

I loved Nicaragua, and I had run my business for a total of three years before I proposed selling it to Jen. That was the longest amount of time I had stayed anywhere other than my childhood home. For me, the time just felt right. I was ready to step away from that project and move onto the next. There's no better way for me to describe the feeling, something just told me it was time to go.

It was hard for me to conceptualize someone else taking over a business I had invested so much of my time, money and, more than anything, myself into. I was worried it would fail or that the part of me that was ingrained in it would fade. I swallowed all the negative possibilities and decided to trust that everything would be okay, and that I needed to continue to grow as a businessperson and a human.

The flight from Houston to Managua was smaller and warmer. I had changed into my sandals before boarding, and I was happy to see I had a window seat again. I liked being able to see how much the world could change in a matter of eight hours. From the rainy skies of San Francisco to the dry, flat earth of Houston to the palm trees and volcanoes of Nicaragua. Those airplane windows had some of the best views I had seen in my life, views that I could not stay away from for long.

This time I was venturing off to a potential new business opportunity in Nicaragua. I had made many connections through opening the hostel, and it helped keep me in the loop of opportunities that were hard to not pursue. Though I had taken a handful of trips back to Nicaragua over the last couple years, this was the first visit where I had a vague idea of being rooted there once again. The other trips were vacations. This one was different.

When I had originally decided to open a business in Nicaragua, I didn't think too many years in the future. To me, I had decided to reside there for, well, whatever concept of "forever" I had in my early twenties. A few years later, my mind started to drift, and the idea of home began to change. I had to listen to that and make a move.

Just because you want to start a business abroad does not mean you are locked to that area for the rest of your life. There's no doubt that it's a big commitment, in a lot of ways one of the biggest you'll ever have. When I decided I was ready to go, I looked into my options. Since

I had created a successful business, I was able to sell it and use the profits to move on to my next adventure.

Getting off the plane in Managua felt familiar and comforting. I picked up my baggage and went through customs with ease before walking outside to find a ride to my hotel. I looked at the crowded bus and thought of my cost-saving vomit nightmare years before. I smiled and picked the taxi this time.

35403435R00107

Made in the USA
San Bernardino, CA
23 June 2016